ALL WHO MINISTER

ALL WHO MINISTER

New Ways of
Serving God's People

Maylanne Maybee
editor

November 18, 2002

To Bridget - a kindred spirit - with many thanks for your hospitality, vision, & passion.

Maylanne

▲ ABC Publishing
ANGLICAN BOOK CENTRE

Published 2001 by
Anglican Book Centre
600 Jarvis Street
Toronto, Ontario M4Y 2J6

Canadian Cataloguing in Publication Data

All who minister: new ways of serving God's people

ISBN 1-55126-341-6

1. Pastoral theology — Case studies. I. Maybee, Maylanne

BV660.3.A44 2001   253   C2001-900868-6

Remember, Lord,
your one holy catholic and apostolic Church,
redeemed by the blood of your Christ.
Reveal its unity, guard its faith,
and preserve it in peace.

Remember all who minister
in your Church.

Book of Alternative Services,
page 210

CONTENTS

INTRODUCTION

Maylanne Maybee

My friend Diane says that all ministry is about encouragement. That's what the essays in this book are meant to do — to encourage those seeking to expand "mainstream" or "normal" forms of ministry, trying new things, forging new paths. Being at the cutting edge can be frustrating, isolating, and confusing. But it's also a place of risk, excitement, and creativity. The case studies that appear in this book are about people who have ventured onto paths of ministry that have not been heavily trodden. Some have done so out of a sense of vision and possibility, others out of economic or demographic necessity, others still out of a prophetic sense of how things ought to be. Most were motivated by a mixture of these reasons.

The selection of stories and case studies in this book is not meant to be definitive or comprehensive, but rather to give a glimpse into what some people in some places are trying and learning, at times through success, at times through failure, usually through both.

For the most part, they are Anglican stories. Despite variations and at times profound differences, Anglicans are shaped by a polity based on scripture, the creeds, the sacraments of baptism and eucharist, and the episcopate as a living human expression of the witness to the resurrection first given by the apostles. Anglicans are informed by Benedictine spirituality that values stability as a quality of community, and humility and servanthood as qualities of leadership. Within Anglicanism, there is tolerance, if not always enthusiasm, for hierarchy and distinction in roles and functions, based on a recognition that the solemn appointment of bishops, presbyters, and deacons is our inherited way of organizing Christian life and community.

These may be some of the givens, but the social context in which the Anglican Church exists in Canada does not resemble what it was a couple of generations ago.* The world has been experiencing major restructuring in its economic arrangements. Social energies have become polarized between global concerns and local or regional interests. Governments have routinely downloaded onto the private and voluntary sectors areas of service that once were considered public responsibilities — education, health care, care for the poor, the homeless, and the dispossessed. Indigenous people in Canada are gaining increasing recognition for their long-standing struggle to achieve justice, both through the honouring of previous agreements and the forging of new social contracts founded on principles of respect and self-determination. Demographic changes are having a major impact on social structures, especially as the population bulge of the postwar baby boom (1945–1960) begins to move into late middle age and approaches retirement age.

The church, and with it the concept and practice of ministry, has been shaken to the core by these winds of change. Canadians have grown indifferent, if not hostile, to the church's presence and role in society. This is partly owing to the exponential growth of religious and cultural pluralism in Canada, and partly to the widespread disenchantment with institutional authority that has followed revelations of sexual abuse and misconduct. Feminist critique has altered the prevailing view of authority and exercise of

---

* I am indebted to Dr. Walter Deller and the Rev. Ansley Tucker for key ideas in this section.

power. Quite different patterns of volunteerism are emerging. At the same time, church membership has been in decline, congregations are ageing, and cradle Anglicanism is becoming a thing of the past.

The Very Rev. Peter Elliott, Dean of New Westminster, has described the shifts in the Canadian church over the last fifty years this way:

> The Church of the Corporate Empire during the 1950s, when the church was at one with the political and economic powers of the time, became The Church of the Democratic Revolution in the 1960s and 1970s, opening up the priesthood to women, involving the laity in liturgy and leadership. We now find ourselves in The Church of Voluntary Discipleship, redefining the boundaries between church and society, and resembling more closely the pre-Constantinian era.

I often hear people talk about "new ways of being church," but in the end, there aren't that many variations. People who assemble for eucharist, who gather for prayer and fellowship, who strive to learn and practise the faith, who offer mutual care and support, and who serve others besides themselves are being church. People who don't do these things aren't! There are, however, many ways of "pushing the envelope," and the stories in this book are about those who are doing so; about people who have inherited a legacy of professionalized ministry and found it wanting; and about their efforts to find alternatives.

The case studies reflect a cross-section of Canada's geographic and cultural realities and the variety of challenges they present — Mutual Ministry in the West Kootenay, ministry formation for Indigenous people in Manitoba and northwestern Ontario, inner city ministry in Vancouver, Ottawa, and Montreal.

In Canada's small rural or extra-urban communities, the challenge is that many can no longer afford the housing and stipend for a full-time seminary graduate. In parts of North America and beyond, the Total or Mutual Ministry movement has offered exciting new directions for congregations and clergy. Dioceses that have adopted this model are employing people with formal theological education as "missioners" to teach, encourage, and coach congregational ministry teams, instead of placing them in situations where they prop up struggling churches and exercise a "one man band" ministry. Congregations are functioning less as hiring committees looking for outside professionals, and more as discernment committees identifying gifts among their own members and designating, supporting, and recognizing people who perform the functions of ministry. When this happens, members of congregations start paying closer attention to the tasks at hand. They start imagining themselves doing the tasks. They pay closer attention to themselves and to their relationship with fellow parishioners, their neighbourhood, their bishop, the wider church. The process is vitalizing. People wake up! They fly by the seat of their pants. They look for something beyond themselves — strength, courage, inspiration. They worry less about mistakes, in themselves and others, and more about doing the work — God's work.

In some of Canada's urban and inner city communities, the challenge is that a one size fits all approach to parish ministry simply doesn't work when the majority of people within the parish boundaries are struggling with major life issues such as survival, health, homelessness, and unemployment. In these situations, churches are faced with a painful dilemma — either toe the line and "succeed" in the same way that a suburban church would, or close the doors and fly against the most compelling of gospel imperatives: "I was hungry and you gave me food, thirsty and you gave me something to drink, a stranger and you welcomed me, naked and you gave me clothing." There are churches and people who choose not to close their doors or move on to someplace else, and their stories of struggle and courage also are about doing God's work.

In Canada's Indigenous communities, the challenge is that a eurocentric model of education and ministry may be not only unaffordable or unsuitable but deeply harmful, as history has shown. In these instances, entirely new ways of forming communities and ministers need to be developed, and the stories of these experiments have been included.

As the church searches for alternatives, the concept of ministry itself comes up as the subject of much discussion, controversy, and confusion. There are some who emphasize that, in the early church, all Christians functioned as ministers through their baptism, and that this practice and understanding should be revived. Others point out that even in New Testament times communities conferred authority on their leadership through prayer and the laying on of hands, and that in every age the church needs to select and authorize official leaders.

Both these positions have something to offer. Ministry is a concept that has universal dimensions. We use it in our public language, for instance, when we refer to ministers of government. "Ministry" comes from a Latin word that has to do with putting oneself in a minus situation. It's about setting aside one's own needs and wants so that others can grow and develop. Practising ministry differs from practising a profession such as law or medicine, which assume a fixed dependency on the part of clients or patients, and a difference in knowledge, power, and status between the one who gives and the one who receives the service. It is precisely the power difference that makes the regulating of professions so important. At its root, ministry is a relationship that moves in the direction of equality without first assuming equality. It aims to build mutuality and friendship between equals. Jesus' parting words to his disciples were, "I do not call you servants any longer, because the servant does not know what the master is doing; but I have called you friends, because I have made known to you everything that I have heard from my Father."

In this sense, the style for practising ministry is to set examples. Ministry is the natural expression of faith in daily life, the natural expression of love and labour. It does not depend on education or knowledge alone, for without faith and vitality, there is no depth and no nuancing of moral value. This style of ministry is not ego-centred or heroic. It is mundane. It shows respect for the work, values, and attitudes of others. Ministry is not transactional: it is not done in order to get something in return, nor to convert another person, nor to deliver specialized information. A minister comes to a relationship or situation with openness to being enriched and changed by the other. If a person has fallen down, ministry is not necessarily simply a matter of pulling him back up, but of quietly being beside him as an act of encouragement until he discovers within himself the strength and resources to get up on his own. Ministry requires humility, obedience, listening, respect, and readiness to set aside one's own needs and perspectives.

For the purposes of this book, however, certain assumptions about ministry are more specific. One is that it continues to be useful to understand ministry as a role or relationship made official in a manner that involves the assent of the local community. There is an element of ministry that is public and representative, and that calls for appropriate forms of recognition and accountability.

Another assumption is that the practice of ministry among baptized Christians can and should be much broader and more varied than the ordained offices. It's not just that plural forms of ministry should be recognized, but that ministry itself is a corporate thing. It belongs not exclusively to ordained persons, nor in lesser form to non-ordained persons, but in a dynamic interaction among all baptized members of a local community (diocese and parish), who hold each other mutually accountable, who respect different gifts and domains for ministry, and who acknowledge important differentials of power, experience, and giftedness within the body of the faithful.

A third assumption is that ministry is about equipping, encouraging, and supporting ordinary Christians to do God's work and to be God's people. It has to do with leading and living our life together as church, and helping mission to happen in ways suited to the context and culture. There is a tendency sometimes automatically to include all aspects of the Christian life under the category of "ministry." I prefer to think of ministry more specifically as "equipping the saints" so that the saints may in turn equip themselves and the world to meet and receive God.

These are stories about being at the edges and working out of mixed motives — which are excellent conditions for the movement of Spirit. So this book is also about how people see the work of the Spirit moving in and transforming the church. Spirit cannot be programmed or coerced, only given a chance. Many of us may long for the church to wake up to its changed place in society, to be re-ignited by the pioneering zeal of its early days, and to embrace new paradigms and directions of ministry. The more we give expression and shape to this longing, the more likely it is that transformation will take place. But in the end, no single conference, book, or experiment will bring about the transformation for which we long — it's a journey, and telling our stories is one important way of encouraging each other on the way.

LOCAL AND SHARED MINISTRY

THE
KOKANEE STORY
Kootenay

Dirk T. Rinehart-Pidcock

Of all the innovations in ministry that have been tried in recent years, the notion of Mutual Ministry (also called Total or Total Common Ministry) has captured the imagination of church communities, especially those that might otherwise have to close or struggle continually just to survive. In those parts of the Anglican Church of Canada where economic, cultural, or demographic conditions have made change a necessity for survival, Mutual Ministry has been tried, reflected on, and adapted. Dirk Rinehart-Pidcock, a former director of the Sorrento Centre, a retreat house and conference centre in BC, was one of its pioneers. "It is my conviction," he reflects, "that Mutual Ministry is closer to what God would have us be than the traditional model, which is so heavily dependent on professional clergy." His story of ministry renewal in the Kokanee Region is a good introduction to the vision of Mutual Ministry and its application in Canada.

The Kokanee Region in the diocese of Kootenay is rugged lovely land that includes two major mountain ranges and three large valley floors graced by extensive lake systems. The mission statement of that region says: "We, the people of the Kokanee Region of the diocese of Kootenay, are a scattered family of parishes located in mountain valleys in the midst of God's natural beauty. As the body of Christ, we are called to serve God in the world by celebrating individual and corporate ministries."

My involvement with the Kokanee Region began in 1991 when I was selected to serve as the coordinator of ministries. It was my mandate to introduce Mutual Ministry and to coordinate various ministries, serving a scattered cluster: six small village churches and one larger church in the city of Nelson, BC, with a population of about 10,000. The original ministry team I worked with included a semi-retired priest responsible for providing pastoral care and leading worship, and a dozen or so licensed lay readers (now called Lay Ministers of Word and Sacrament).

The vision of Mutual or Total Ministry emerged as a way of understanding ministry and shaping church life in the 1960s in the diocese of Alaska, under Bishop Bill Gordon. It then found its way to the diocese of Nevada, where some remarkable work in ministry development had been underway for a number of years.

My own commitment to this vision of ministry was strengthened in 1980, when I invited Bishop Wes Frensdorff of Nevada to lead a summer course on Total Ministry at Sorrento Centre. Participants remember his keen mind, passion, and outrageous humour. Frensdorff drew significant ideas from the writings of Roland Allen, a Church of England missionary in China during the early 1900s, who was a severe critic of the missionary methods of his day. Allen proposed a radical rediscovery of the methods of St. Paul, who left behind him empowered communities of faith that were truly indigenous, blessed with leadership for worship and service, and able to carry on the work of the gospel. None of these leaders had been professionally trained. All were volunteers. All received on the job training. Allen sought to reclaim the understanding of the church as the body of Christ, in which the gifts of each member are valued and affirmed. He promoted the need for volunteer priests so that the sacraments might be consistently available to the faithful. His radical thought was a scandal in its day, but some fifty years later resurfaced in Alaska, Nevada, and beyond.

Frensdorff presented Total Ministry not as a tinkering with existing structures but as a radical reorientation to our very understanding of church. He dreamed of the church as "a ministering community" rather than "a community gathered around a minister." His assumption was that each baptized person has a vocation and is gifted by God for ministry, and every community of faith has within it the resources needed for ministry and mission. Congregations are empowered to identify and select leaders from among themselves, including potential priests and deacons for local ministry. Professional clergy become primarily equippers and mentors rather than doers of ministry. Mutual Ministry is both holistic and radical. It provides a truly alternative model of ministry for the church.

Kootenay's Bishop Berry had suggested that the idea be introduced into the Kokanee Region at a time of discouragement and decline. Reaction among the congregations was mixed. Some felt that the scheme was being imposed from outside as the only option in a situation of need. Others were apprehensive lest too much be demanded of them, but after realizing what was expected, several lay leaders became committed to the vision. A generous grant from the Lily Foundation made it possible to begin implementation, now under the leadership of Bishop David Crawley.

Upon arriving, I was surprised to discover that my primary task, besides building relationships of trust, was to introduce the vision throughout the region and convince people of its worth. I soon came to realize that many Anglicans are far more emotionally, psychologically, and spiritually wedded to a clergy centred church than Mutual Ministry envisages.

I learned that effective ministry development requires significant teaching that involves all members of the parish community. People need to be captured by the vision of what it means to belong to the *laos*, the people of God, the body of Christ, the baptized community. Much of the initial teaching needs to be based on St. Paul's powerful insights of the church expressed in 1 Corinthians 12, Romans 12, and Ephesians 4. People also need to know how far the church has drifted! For many generations, Anglicans and other historic churches have lived in systems that are "top down" and clergy centred. Ministers in this framework are clergy, period. It requires a major shift in thinking for people to see that this dominant system is a grave distortion. Many were and are happy with this distortion. It became important for me to remember that change happens gradually, and that the recovery process will continue for several generations.

Out of this teaching and learning emerged the Discovery Process, a tool for helping the congregations to clarify ministry needs and opportunities, both within and beyond the church, to identify leadership positions, and to nominate people for those positions. The outcome was the formation of ministry support teams. Members of the ministry support teams were selected to give support and leadership to the ministries of all the baptized, not to claim these ministries only for themselves. In most instances, the selection was clear. In a few cases when it was not, a second round of nominations was required. Feelings were sometimes hurt when individuals were not nominated to the team, or were not nominated to the particular position they desired. Once nominated, teams came into being, and began to meet monthly for study, team building, prayer, and orientation. Their education and formation was enhanced by additional workshops and study opportunities, including week-long commitments at Sorrento Centre.

Early on, five individuals were sent to the USA to be trained as Stephen Leaders as part of a rich ecumenical program in pastoral care. Upon returning home, these five people facilitated workshops and training throughout the region, equipping others to be more effective in their caring ministries.

By 1996, three ministry support teams were ready for commissioning and ordaining. The teams included twenty-five persons to be commissioned, as well as four priests and two deacons to be ordained. They belonged to the parishes of St. Saviour, Nelson, the largest of the Kokanee parishes; to St. Matthew, South Slocan, the smallest; and to St. Mark, Kaslo, a village church.

The Mutual Ministry journey took the people of the Kokanee Region in unexpected directions. An event of critical importance occurred when a delegation of Kokanee people visited the Seven Rivers Cluster in the dioceses of Eastern Oregon and Idaho. The work of Mutual Ministry had been underway in this cluster for several years, and the combination of mentoring and hospitality they extended made all the difference in encouraging the Kokanee delegation to press on. It is essential for those involved in new initiatives to link with others for wisdom and support wherever possible. At present the diocese of Northern Michigan provides mentoring to many throughout North America and beyond.

Mutual Ministry seems to me best suited to small village parishes without resident professional clergy, though my experience is limited. All seven parishes in the Kokanee Region have moved significantly towards becoming ministering communities in which all members claim and exercise ministry. The reasons are complex why four parishes have not yet chosen to embrace an intentional expresssion of Mutual Ministry. All are small congregations of primarily older parishioners. For some congregations, there has been a lack of energy for major local development and an inability to believe in themselves. Some could not imagine that a priest for local ministry could be identified from their midst. Two or three of these parishes may yet respond to the challenge, and others may sadly not survive.

At the best of times, I understand the church to be in a long-term recovery process. The principles of Mutual Ministry are not an arbitrary passing fad without depth or consequence, but are about reclaiming the soul of the church. The church, as institution, is under great stress in our day. Is it possible, as Douglas Hall suggests in *The Future of the Church*, that God is humbling us? Is it possible that much has to die before a new reality can be born? Verna Dozier's opening words in *The Authority of the Laity* have captured my heart: "A funny thing happened on the way to the Kingdom. The church, the people of God, became the church, the institution." Mutual Ministry is overwhelmingly about the people of God agenda.

I close with a vivid memory from a Partners-in-Mission consultation in the early 1970s. One of the overseas partners was a bishop from Kenya. His feedback to the host, the Episcopal Church of the USA, included this insight: "North Americans believe they have to be fully prepared, educated, and trained before they can begin; but in Kenya, we begin and discover what we need to learn in order to proceed."

This connects with a powerful Quaker insight: "Proceed as the way opens."

Those of us committed to the Mutual Ministry enterprise are strengthened by this wisdom.

NON-STIPENDIARY ORDAINED MINISTRY

Nova Scotia

David Fletcher

In 1992, the then bishop of Nova Scotia and Prince Edward Island, the Rt. Rev. Arthur Peters, advised the synod of the diocese that he was initiating a pilot project for non-stipendiary ordained ministry. This news was not particularly well received at the time. The clergy were suspicious about issues of competence, and the laity were suspicious about the role and function of the locally ordained. Now, ten years later, many of the initial fears and suspicions have proven unfounded, and we have discovered that the locally ordained have brought renewed vigour and energy to the community of the baptized.

When we began, there were no guidelines — not even a name — for self-supporting clergy. There was no process for selection or affirmation of candidates, no education or formation program, no stipulations about licensing and placement. We also discovered a tremendous naiveté about the ministry of the baptized. "Father knows best" was the general attitude to parish ministry in the diocese.

As we moved towards developing a program for local ordination, it became clear that we needed to be in touch with others engaged in similar ministries. A survey of the Canadian church in

1994 suggested that there was little experience to draw on, so we began networking with dioceses in the Episcopal Church of the USA. The pattern in ECUSA was to regenerate locally ordained clergy through national church canons and diocesan licensing, and to provide training by means of a diocesan school or reading program. Other denominations referred to non-stipendiary clergy as "tentmakers," the trade by which Paul supported himself, or as "self-supporting assistants." We had read about non-stipendiary ministry in the United Kingdom that was closer to the pattern we were trying to develop, and were especially helped by the example in the diocese of Lichfied, where lay readers and non-stipendiary clergy are both provided for in a comprehensive program for local ministry development. We also looked at the work of the Roman Catholic Church in developing a non-stipendiary vocational diaconate.

An early decision was made to label our program Non-Stipendiary Ordained Ministry (NSOM), recognizing that all the baptized are expected to be engaged in unpaid ministries, and that the ordained have a particular function within the community of the baptized. Since it was not our intention that non-stipendiary clergy should become rectors of parishes, and since some people feared that they might, we specified that only parishes that had a self-supporting ordained ministry already established (either a rector or other supervising clergy) could participate in the program. We also recognized that regional ministries in some areas of the diocese were already developing, and that the locally ordained might well be part of such a ministry development initiative.

Gentle reminders that non-stipendiary clergy were already present in the diocese — clergy who had retired or were working in secular employment — helped to dispel misgivings. Soon it became evident that the quality of the candidates themselves would be the best commendation possible for the program's success.

During that first year, a steering committee and program coordinator were appointed. They held conversations with the local theological college and interviews with those involved in the program and also those most opposed to it. They began to establish a core curriculum, formation activities, and criteria for candidate selection.

The bishop expected that candidates for ordination would have a knowledge of scripture, liturgy, church history, systematic theology, and the practical exercise of ministry. The Atlantic School of Theology was reluctant to offer its three-year continuing education diploma program to persons seeking ordination because it was designed as a lay training program. Consequently, we elected to offer the Thorneloe University certificate in theology and the Education for Ministry program (EFM) as fulfilling the basic requirements of the core curriculum.

We were concerned that candidates seeking ordination should formulate their vocation differently from those trained in seminary. A traditional seminary program takes candidates from their own situation and challenges them with a variety of opportunities for academic learning, spiritual development, and psychological growth. The hoped-for result is self-aware and spiritually mature persons who can be assigned to a parish by themselves where they will be the sole administrative, liturgical, and pastoral authority (and never return to their own home parish except as a guest). In our local ordination program, by contrast, we are fostering people's vocations within their own faith community, intentionally focusing on collegiality and on developing persons who will provide supplementary and supportive ministries within their own congregation or region.

In the traditional pattern, candidates for ordination are self-selected. They generally make an appointment with their rector or bishop to say that they feel called to ordained ministry. Then they they begin a process of assessment and academic theological education. The parish role is minimal, partly because everyone knows that the candidate will not return to active ministry in the home parish.

As we began developing an affirmation process for those to be ordained locally, it became clear that the relationships between the candidate and the incumbent (usually a rector), and between the candidate and the congregation were critically important. Candidates were identified, commended, and affirmed within the faith community. The formation activities in the NSOM program now include a biannual conference for the parish representatives and rectors, as well as the candidates and locally ordained themselves. We tried to avoid the terminology of "raising up" candidates (i.e., putting them "over" the community of faith).

When a parish indicates its desire to include non-stipendiary deacons or priests, Sunday sermons and presentations to the parish council or vestry are scheduled to begin a teaching process with the congregation. Vocational workshops for potential candidates emphasize the baptismal covenant rather than ordination, because we want to challenge individuals to examine a variety of ministries within the church, not simply ordination.

By 1997, many candidates were using the Atlantic School of Theology's diploma program (despite the original intentions of the school). Others were enrolled in EFM or the Thorneloe Diploma programs. Certificates in pastoral care, or a unit of parish-based clinical pastoral education, and weekend formation events three times per year, rounded out the typical pattern of preordination training.

Five years into the program, we began to see where it worked well and where we had more work to do. When a new incumbent came to a parish with locally ordained clergy or candidates for local ordination, the transition was not always smooth. There were issues of collegiality and work expectations. It was also important to consider spouses and significant others whose role in parish life might change along with their partners' role. Now, formation events that include spouses have become a part of our NSOM program. We have learned the need to encourage participants to balance commitments to family, work, and church life, and to be clear with colleagues in ministry about these priorities.

Deployment issues arise when there are long-term pastoral

vacancies in the diocese, and when parishes cannot afford full-time rectors. For example, a non-stipendiary priest was appointed as a part-time interim in a parish with a job description more like that of a rector, yet the honorarium that was offered did not include a benefits package. This clearly was outside the intentions of the non-stipendiary program, as well as a violation of the Guidelines for Fair Employment Practices of the church.

The larger picture, however, is encouraging. The NSOM program now involves more than thirty individuals, and is functioning in every region of the diocese. A rigorous process for moving from non-stipendiary into stipendiary ordained ministry is in place, to discourage the perception that the NSOM candidates will become rectors of parishes. Lay Christian education, especially through EFM, is growing, and there is an increasing understanding that many different gifts may be offered for ministry.

Having been privileged to make presentations about the NSOM program in our diocese on many occasions, I offer the following observations. The candidates' deep roots and commitments to the communities in which they live give tremendous integrity to their ministry. Many who are being identified as non-stipendiary clergy today would have been unable to act upon a perceived call twenty-five or thirty years ago because of family commitments, educational requirements, occupational endeavours, or gender, and have found that local ordination answers the persistent longing that they have felt regarding a call to ordained ministry. We have attempted to provide a well-rounded education and formation program to prepare candidates to work as associate priests in liturgical (presiding and preaching) and pastoral ministries. We have also worked to foster a clearer understanding of diaconal ministry and the development of a community of deacons.

I close with a metaphor. Compare the orchid and the hedge-rose. Both are blossoming flowers. The orchid requires constant care, needs to be handled delicately, and will shrivel and die if not tended properly (especially if it gets cold or doesn't get enough light or nutrients). On the other hand, the hedge-rose is deep-rooted and hardy, blooming where it is planted and tenacious enough to thrive in spite of what goes on around it. As a seminary-trained full-time rector myself, I recognize something of the orchid in my own ministry. At the same time, I have seen the beauty and life of the hedge-rose in the ministry of the locally ordained, and rejoice that both can exist together within the greater garden of the community of the baptized that we call the church.

Lay Leadership Comes Alive

The Greater Parish of Oxbow Qu'Appelle

Michelle Moore

The Greater Parish of Oxbow is a rural multi-point parish where distances are great and congregations are small and ageing. Its last rector was a "one man band" who lived at least thirty miles away and had little to do with the communities outside of the one in which he lived. Services were held once or twice a month. Lay participation was limited to setting up the altar for communion, playing the organ, or taking up the collection. The ladies' guild and the occasional Sunday school or confirmation class were the only organized activities of the parish. Many people were unaware that there was an Anglican church in the community. Between rectors, the church doors closed and parishioners sat with folded hands waiting for the bishop to send another priest. Every few years we would be shifted to a different parish — an experience that led to a strong sense of congregationalism but that left little opportunity to bond with the larger parish.

In 1979, one such shift left us "welded" to a parish to the south, thus forming a nine-point parish that covered 2,500 square miles, making a round trip of 165 miles. Apart from the rector, we had little in common with the other churches in the parish. Attempts at promoting a feeling of unity failed. The parish council consisted of representatives from nine very separate congregations whose struggle for survival left little desire to get to know or care about each other. Our last rector appointed a local church member as chair of the parish council, an innovative move that later proved to be invaluable. When the rector announced his resignation, it was apparent that we could no longer afford a traditional clergy appointment. Concerned parishioners met with the bishop to discuss ways of continuing without clergy.

We agreed that the first priority was to continue an uninterrupted schedule of church services, and that education of local leaders was essential for this to happen. Parish members began leading morning and evening prayer with minimal instruction, and sacraments were celebrated by "borrowing" priests — one from a neighbouring parish, one from retirement. The parish council executive handled the administration — no easy task in such a widespread parish.

Years of conditioning in which all aspects of church life were controlled by ordained seminary-trained clergy led us to assume that local parishioners who had no formal training could not be left in charge. Yet the sort of education that was required — something that could be delivered to parishioners on their home ground and at an appropriate time (avoiding seedtime and harvest, and work, family, and community commitments) could not be put together overnight.

We found ourselves learning on the job by trial and error. We read the rubrics repeatedly. With the help of a diocesan grant, we started a parish library, and our personal libraries began to grow as we struggled to learn how to lead services better and to understand Anglicanism.

Not surprisingly, as our involvement grew, the Anglican Church became more visible in a community where other denominations were represented by seminary-trained ordained clergy. Suddenly, our church was no longer the rector; it was us, and we felt woefully inadequate for this role. At every opportunity we would corner unsuspecting clergy and fire questions at them until they begged for mercy or escaped us! When we had a chance to attend a service other than our own, we sat at the front of the church and watched the priest intently to see how things were done, then asked after the service about what we didn't understand.

The clergy did not at first understand this need. We were gently told that leading worship reverently was more important than doing it right. Requests for constructive criticism were met with praise rather than suggestions. We were told that even seminary trained clergy didn't have all the right answers. Our response was that they could get away with a lot more because they were acknowledged experts — professionally trained, in clerical collar, and coming from more than twenty miles away. We were trying to be church leaders in towns where people had known our families for generations. They knew every mistake we'd made, every success we'd ever had, what we did for a living, how we had spent last Saturday night and with whom. How do you minister to people you have grown up with? To parents of your friends? To your teachers? You must interact with the same people, not just in church life but at work and at social events. Even Jesus had a tough time in his home town. If things got really difficult, we couldn't just resign, pack up the farm, and move on down the road.

Because we were a novelty — a "do it yourself" parish — we were invited to speak at synod, to other parishes, to a neighbouring diocese, to a provincial ministry conference. We embraced such opportunities, feeling that it was important to share our story in the hope that others could learn from our successes and not have to repeat our mistakes. Our message to churches everywhere, despite size or financial status, is that encouraging parishioners to be informed and actively involved leads them to greater enthusiasm and commitment, and results in a stronger more vibrant church.

Our diocese was committed to identifying, enhancing, and celebrating the ministry of all the baptized. To this end, a special staff position for a ministries development coordinator was created. Gradually, the longed-for education became available —

workshops on Anglicanism, church history and tradition, liturgy and worship, Bible study, pastoral care. The fact that we were living out these ministries before being trained for them was not what we would have wished, but all things work together for good. A ministry support team, comprising five parish leaders, three of whom had been identified as potential candidates for local ordination, met every couple of months for further education. An Education for Ministry (EFM) group also met regularly. Other worship leaders attended some educational events but were generally satisfied with things as they were. Eventually, seven worship coordinators were commissioned — an important recognition and affirmation of the ministry we shared.

In the seven years following the rector's departure, we kept our doors open. Services were held more frequently. We initiated a parish newsletter, and annual parish picnics were well attended. We became one parish family. Our concern for each other was particularly evident at budget meetings.

We now have a core of hardworking and dedicated parish leaders, some of whom have gone on to become involved at the diocesan, provincial, and national levels of the church. This has meant a major commitment of time and energy — often more time is spent on the road than at meetings — but it has provided us with valued opportunities to learn more about our church, to take part in decision making, and to deepen our understanding of the needs of the truly small congregation (seven to twenty members, for example, not all communicants, meeting in a small church building without running water or adequate heat, in a town with a population of 400).

On the minus side, we have not been able to find Sunday school or confirmation curricula that work for us. An attempt to move parish council meetings around the parish to encourage local involvement failed. Despite our involvement in the wider church, it is difficult to motivate others in the parish to get involved beyond the four walls of their own church. In a parish where the only qualification for a job is to be willing to try, the most active leaders verge on over-commitment and run the risk of burnout.

The depopulation of rural Saskatchewan continues, as do the escalating problems of life on a small farm. Many of our congregations are getting older and smaller and poorer. Regardless of what the future holds, we have grown in the knowledge and love of Jesus Christ. That has left us richer as individuals and as a community, as Anglicans and as Christians, as creatures of God's creation.

PARISHES WITHOUT FULL-TIME CLERGY
The Parish of Raymore Qu'Appelle

Robin Duffield

"Is there life outside Toronto, Montreal, and Vancouver?" asks Robin Duffield of the parish of Raymore, in the diocese of Qu'Appelle. "You bet there is!" The parish, situated 120 kilometres north of Regina in southcentral Saskatchewan, has existed since the early 1900s. It has four points — Raymore, Semans, Punnichy, and Kutawa. It has been served by twenty-five clergy and seven bishops.

. . .

Our first experience without a full-time priest was during 1988–89. Over the previous several years, the incumbent had encouraged members of the various congregations to participate in services led in their own churches by local parishioners. When we were left without a full-time priest, the stage was set to run the parish ourselves. The diocese of Qu'Appelle arranged to have a priest come twice a month for communion services in Raymore Parish and the neighbouring Parish of the Cree People. In order to save the priest from having to travel to all four points of the parish, a joint service was held in Raymore. The fellowship time after the service allowed members of the different points to get to know each other better, although we had already become acquainted through working together in community organizations, as well as through joint services for special occasions. As we jelled into a church community, we came to realize that if we cooperated, and if we had to, we could manage without a full-time priest.

In the summer of 1989, we did obtain a full-time priest, but by 1991 the parish realized that we could no longer afford a full-time priest and still meet our other responsibilities. We arranged with the local archdeacon, from the Parish of the Cree People, to celebrate the eucharist at Raymore when his schedule would allow it.

Because we already had some idea of what parish life would be like without a full-time priest, it wasn't such a scary prospect to take over the services ourselves. We also knew that it was up to us to keep the church going. Out on the prairie, if you wait for someone else to do it, it doesn't get done! We have the highest per capita rate of volunteerism in Canada, and it felt good to know that we could do it without lapsing into helpless dependency.

In the early 1990s, the diocese began to integrate us into the newly established Discovery Process, a model based roughly on work being done in Northern Michigan. (There, a structured format, called a Covenant Group Process, has been developed to lead a congregation through a formation period, culminating in a commissioning service to affirm the ministry of all the baptized, and to license and ordain a ministry support team.) With the help of a diocesan coordinator, parishes are encouraged to raise up their own leaders and ministers through a process of discernment and training.

Letters were sent to all members of the congregation requesting the names of those they believed could put their talents towards administration, music, education, pastoral care, and other facets of ministry. Workshops were then set up by the diocese to help us with areas of ministry in which we were not strong, and to help people overcome their shyness about taking a front and centre role. The classes were open to all members of the congregation, not only to those whose names had been put forward through the

Discovery Process. Everyone was given a part to play in the success of the church. The Discovery Process offered the possibility of designating one or more persons for local ordination, though in our case, this was not a strong expectation. We did, however, expect that the process would result in stronger parish leadership, and that an arrangement would be made with a visiting priest to come celebrate the eucharist.

As the rural areas of Canada become depopulated, we must look at all the options available to us. Since early 1994, we have been working with the Lutheran congregation in Quinton, a small village ten kilometres east of Raymore. Quinton is facing the same challenges we did in 1991. We have been sharing ideas with them, as well as joint communion services at either Quinton or Raymore, with a time of fellowship after each service.

We do not believe that we are unique in the way we have approached our situation. The four points of Raymore Parish have always gotten along well together, even though there may be differences of opinion from time to time. Everyone's opinion is considered important. Whether the rectory, which is now being rented out, needs a new coat of paint or a service needs to be led, members of the congregation will get to it, and the work will be done without fuss or bother.

Raymore Parish had few problems in making the transition from being a clergy led parish. From the beginning, we always had a voice in how the parish was run. We weren't afraid to ask questions and look for answers. We also felt that if we didn't try, we wouldn't know whether we could succeed. We were not afraid of failing, because no matter what happened, we could learn from the experience.

Above all, we have learned to keep a sense of humour. A good laugh at our own foibles can certainly make the whole situation seem less daunting. We have also learned not to let pride get in the way of delegating tasks and sharing the load. In this way, a few aren't left to suffer burnout. We have two organists, three liturgical leaders, someone to organize and phone readers, two licensed communion assistants, and about ten people to lead the prayers of the people. We have an efficient secretary-treasurer, very active churchwardens, and a dedicated ACW. Two members of the parish publish a quarterly newsletter with items from all points in the parish, cartoons, and when possible, a covering article from the local archdeacon. Keeping the congregation informed is an important aspect of our success. If people feel they don't know what's going on, they soon lose interest and stop attending altogether.

Other parishes in our diocese are now doing what Raymore has done. Often we have been asked why we succeeded, and I'm not really sure what the answer is. We had a job to do and we did it! Perhaps it was the influence of the prairie pioneers. We did what we did best: we cooperated. We cooperated when the Saskatchewan Wheat Pool was formed, when a skating rink was needed for the local community, and when the church needed to be built. We're still cooperating today. It's not hard and it doesn't hurt a bit. The trick is to give everyone a job and let them do it. You might be surprised at just what talents have been hidden all those years.

. . .

Tragically, Robin Duffield died of cancer in December 2000. A subsequent conversation with Josephine Richardson, who with her husband is one of the worship leaders in Raymore, indicates that things are continuing much as Robin has told. As the tone of the article suggests, there is a strong sense of independence among the people of Raymore. As they were making the transition to becoming a self-managed parish, the interventions of the diocesan office were not always welcome, and some tension resulted. There are still those who prefer the way things are without seeking further responsibility or involvement, and those who wish to continue to grow and learn in the faith, taking advantage of the certificate program offered by the diocese.

Interest in the possibility of local ordination is not strong. The regional archdeacon comes in two or three times a month to preside at the eucharist, and is also available for weddings and funerals. When he is not there, a service booklet is used, based on an expanded version of morning prayer from the Book of Alternative Services. *Sermons are prepared with the help of the Internet, where texts based on the lectionary are posted, sent out in batches, and edited! Except when farmwork demands it, Sunday attendance is steady at between twenty and twenty-five people. The greatest challenge is the declining number of families with small children and the tendency of younger people to move away.*

Ecumenical Shared Ministry

St. Peter's Ecumenical Church
Slave Lake, Athabasca

George Pell

St. Peter's Ecumenical Church is a shared ministry of the Anglican, Evangelical Lutheran, and United churches in the resource community of Slave Lake on the fringe of Northern Alberta.

The town of Slave Lake is one of several settlements that were established on the southern shores of Lesser Slave Lake, connected by the CP Railway as it forged its way west towards the Rockies. There had been an Indigenous community, Sawridge, at the southeastern end of Lesser Slave Lake, but after being flooded out in the 1930s, it was moved to higher ground and developed into the present town of Slave Lake. Incorporated as a village in 1961 with a population of 450, Slave Lake is now a town of 7,000 (half under twenty-six years of age) with paved streets, modern recreational facilities and educational opportunities, a wonderful 25-kilometre-long white sand beach, and good prospects for the future. For Indigenous and non-Indigenous residents, including those whose employment brings them to the area for a few years, Slave Lake has been a model of cooperative living and working.

Although many congregations are now considering some form of ecumenical shared ministry because of population shifts or economic concerns — as well as the move towards full communion between the Anglican and Lutheran churches in Canada that was agreed to in the summer of 2001— shared ministry has existed since the 1970s in Slave Lake, Alberta. St. Peter's was born of desire, not necessity, and has been nurtured by a shared experience of the vitality that this type of ministry can create.

Anglican ministry in the Slave Lake area began in 1910, with clergy visiting by train. In the 1930s, a United church was built in the nearby community of Kinuso, and an Anglican church in Slave Lake. Other United and Anglican churches were established in surrounding areas in the 1950s. By the 1970s, all three denominations that would become St. Peter's Ecumenical Church were active in Slave Lake. Anglicans had a resident priest but lost their building when a grocery chain purchased their property. Lutherans were being served by a lay minister appointed by LAMP (Lutheran Association of Missionary Pilots) and the Missouri Synod of the Lutheran Church. A United Church congregation had been constituted, served by a lay minister, and was meeting in a school.

In 1976, not long after organic union between the Anglican and United churches had failed on a national level, Slave Lake United Church joined with the Anglican parish. In the same year, the Lutheran minister stepped down and encouraged the congregation to join with the Anglicans for worship. Lutherans officially joined the shared ministry in 1978, and in 1987 were constituted as an official congregation of what would become the Evangelical Lutheran Church in Canada.

From the beginning of this shared ministry, the desire was to respect the unique history and traditions that Anglicans, Lutherans, and United Church members brought into this new venture, and also to seek a common life of worship, study, and service. Together, they built a new church building in 1981 on lands owned by the Anglican Church. The congregation, currently facing the need to expand the building, has reaffirmed its commitment to work and worship together.

The first clergyperson was an Anglican, who was also appointed by the United Church as an ordained supply minister. Since then, clergy of each denomination have served this shared ministry. However, there has never been a set term or a sequence of choosing pastors from the three denominations. The desire of the parish is to choose the candidate who can best contribute to the unique complex ministry of St. Peter's Ecumenical Church. When a minister leaves, the denomination of that clergyperson is responsible for supply or interim ministry until the next pastor is appointed. A congregational search committee is formed, with equal representation from all three churches, to prepare a parish profile and to solicit and interview candidates. After the committee has agreed on a candidate, the person's name is presented to the membership at large for their concurrence. The appropriate adjudicator from the denomination of the intended pastor is then contacted, and the appointment is made according to the custom of the candidate's denomination. The other two denominational bodies must approve the proposed appointment and, following the appointment, will normally license the person to serve their denominational members within the parish. Beyond the parish level, the pastor is expected to be involved in his or her own denominational courts or synods, and to maintain a "reasonable" connection with the other two churches.

St. Peter's strives to be a "trinity in unity." Three formally constituted congregations make up St. Peter's Ecumenical Church: St. Peter's Anglican Parish, Faith Lutheran Church, and the Slave Lake Pastoral Charge (Slave Lake United Church and Kinuso United Church). One pastor serves all members who make this shared ministry their church family. There is one church board, with three representatives of each denomination and one representative for the "others" who contribute to the life of our parish. Most members attend services of whatever tradition is being followed that week. The only time that denominational clusters meet is at the annual congregational meeting, when representatives to church bodies beyond the parish need to be chosen, or other specific issues or concerns need to be addressed. Working together with other local churches is often more effective than trying to coordinate programs of one denomination, since parishes may be stretched over distances of 100 kilometres or more. Most members at St. Peter's find that there is as much variety in preference and attitude among various churches of their "home" denomination as there is within our parish. They also find that, when issues emerge within a particular church at national or regional levels, members of other churches may be able to look at the issues more objectively, and offer insights and personal support.

In our choice of style for Sunday worship, St. Peter's has never attempted to create a common liturgy. Rather, we rotate the services from week to week, drawing one week from an Anglican prayer book, another time from the Lutheran tradition, and the next from United Church sources. Our practice is to choose elements from the various traditions that find resonance in the other churches' liturgies, and to choose a "common order" to help worshippers feel at home, no matter which liturgy is being followed. Currently we celebrate communion twice a month, a compromise between the typical Anglican practice of weekly communion, the United practice of monthly communion, and Lutheran practice, which can vary from weekly to monthly. We use both grape juice and wine at each celebration of Holy Communion, again respecting the various traditions of our constituent denominations. Music, a source of unity and vitality for us, is drawn from Anglican, Lutheran, and United hymn books and other contemporary sources. The intended rotation doesn't always work perfectly — for example, special days and special guests may require rearranging things. There is more work involved in preparing a variety of forms of worship than in following the traditions of any one denomination or creating a common liturgy. However, we experience the riches of three traditions, and we are required to look closely at what we mean by "Anglican" or "Lutheran" or "United" worship. When visiting elsewhere or moving to a community where their "home" denomination is not present, our members are comfortable in worshipping in other churches. Perhaps our pattern of worship leads to greater respect for our brothers and sisters in Christ, and also to a better appreciation of our own roots.

The family life of our church is likely typical of churches in any of our constituent denominations. Our church school curriculum is selected by the coordinators and the Christian education committee. Study courses are chosen by members or leaders. Local outreach projects reflect the gifts and needs found in our community. One area where choices need to be made is in denominational programs. While there is a great deal of sharing and coordination at various levels, each denomination has its own approach to stewardship, mission, youth, membership, and study. It is an ongoing privilege to receive a variety of options for our church life, but also a challenge to maintain a focus and not to be overwhelmed by the volume or variety offered us.

We are often overwhelmed by paper, since we receive, of course, three sets of denominational mailings, and copies of mailings from outside sources (catalogues, workshops, curriculum offers, etc.) often come in triplicate. At one time, each denomination asked for annual reports of church statistics and church life, using different forms with different questions that called for different combinations of information. Happily for us, a single form for shared ministry parishes has recently been developed.

From time to time, one of the denominations presents a regional or national program as one in which each church "must" or "should" be involved. For us, this is not always possible. Sometimes we feel "outside" the program being promoted, and sometimes we choose not to participate because of "program weariness." We try to maintain a clear sense of the unique situation and ministry of St. Peter's Ecumenical Church, and to communicate that to the various church bodies.

Shared ministry *is* a viable option in many situations. It will work best when it begins with a free and conscious choice to enter this covenant. It will work best when an effort is made to share common concerns and hopes with other ecumenical ministries. It will work best when denominational ties and traditions can be treated as gifts and opportunities to be received, and used to create and enhance a congregation's unique life and ministry. For those of us at St. Peter's, it has been a good choice. After twenty-five years, we can only look forward to the challenges and gifts of the next twenty-five years.

THE
BORDER PARISH
Quebec, Vermont,
and New Hampshire

Granvyl G. Hulse, Jr.

The Border Parish IS a three-mission cluster consisting of All Saints, Hereford, in the province of Quebec; St. Paul's in Canaan, Vermont; and St. Stephen's in Colebrook, New Hampshire.

This geographical area, often referred to as "isolated," is at the headwaters of the Connecticut River in a mountain-ringed valley that once was a pre-Ice Age lake. To the north, beyond the ridge that marks its upper limits, lie the flat plains of southern Quebec. To the east are the vast forests of Maine. To the south and west are the White Mountains of New Hampshire and the Green Mountains of Vermont. As the early inhabitants established their roots, four villages grew up as centres of commerce. The largest, Colebrook, New Hampshire, lies at the juncture of the Mohawk and Connecticut rivers at the southern end of the valley. The next largest settlement comprises the twin villages of Canaan, Vermont, and West Stewartstown, New Hampshire. They are situated to the north of Colebrook and lie opposite each other on the banks of the Connecticut River. The last and smallest of the four villages is Pittsburg, New Hampshire. It is situated at the headwaters of the Connecticut, around the edges of three major lakes. Finally, the settlement of Hereford comprises a long stretch of farms in the hills on the Quebec side of the border, above the village of Canaan. Many of our parishioners have relatives in each of the five settlements, making the Border Parish truly a "family" cluster.

Though it is recorded in the *New Hampshire Diocesan Journal* of 1822 that the Prayer Book was read each Sunday in Colebrook by a "respectable lay gentleman," it was actually missionary priests from the Anglican Church of Canada who first brought the Prayer Book into the valley. Through their efforts, and those of seminary students from Bishop's College in Sherbrooke, Quebec, two small congregations were formed, and in time two churches were constructed. The "elder sister," All Saints, Hereford, was built in 1865, and the next, St. Paul's, was erected in 1900 in Canaan. The last Episcopal missionary probe into the upper Connecticut came with the advent of train service in the late 1800s. Around the turn of the century a priest from Island Pond, Vermont, rode the rails, and established a third congregation from among the Anglican and Episcopal families in Colebrook. The diocese of New Hampshire was able to build on the Vermont effort, and in 1912, the foundation was laid for the construction of St. Stephen's.

Once all three structures were completed, the financial problems associated with small family churches immediately surfaced. Separately, none of the three congregations was capable of supporting a resident minister; none was willing to close its doors and combine with the others; and even if they had merged, all three congregations together did not have the ability to provide a minister with even a basic salary. As such, there was never more than one diocesan supported priest in the area at one time (often none at all), and all three churches came either to rely on whatever seminary trained resources became available to one of the other two, or to use their own lay readers for morning prayer. One result of our being on our own so much is that we developed a preference for morning prayer. Eucharistic services, when they occurred, were not critical to our church life.

Beginning in 1948, a formal cluster program was initiated with the financial responsibility for a resident priest being pro-rated among the three dioceses. This arrangement continued until 1972, when it became apparent that the growth of the three congregations would never be such that they would be able to continue without outside financial assistance. The possibility of locally selected and supported ministry was given serious consideration, and under the direction of the Rev. David Brown, a canon missioner from the diocese of Vermont, a study was made of the three churches to determine the available number of parishioners who would be willing to commit themselves to some form of ministry. Happily, about a dozen men and women stepped forward, and as a result, a team ministry program was selected. In 1974, we received our last full-time priest, the Rev. Robert Leather, who with the canon missioner began to recruit and train those local individuals to take the former's place. Three busy years later, following the ordination of our first priest, a local team ministry was formally inaugurated under the supervision of the priest from the neighbouring Greater Parish of Coaticook.

David Brown's concept of our form of local team ministry accepted certain basics. Each church would still remain independent as far as its vestry, Sunday school, and related housekeeping and maintenance projects were concerned. The ministerial functions, on the other hand, would be the responsibility of what would be called the administrative team. Basically, the team would consist of a seminary trained mentor, and those who had responsibility for leading the worship and performing other ministerial duties such as marriages, baptisms, and funerals, necessary to the life of a congregation. The duties of a full-time priest were chopped up into different elements: the "sacramentalist" (locally ordained) was responsible for sacramental leadership, the preacher for preaching, and the lay reader for the prayers of the people and other parts of the service book. Others were selected to visit, do outreach, and so forth. Since all held full-time jobs outside the church, it was beyond their capabilities, practically, to carry out the normal duties expected of a stipendiary priest. The administrative team was to be a self-contained unit, having its own operating budget (in 1999, about $1,500 US annually) funded in equal measure by the three missions. None of the team would be paid.

David Brown then set four basic guidelines under which the team would operate.

First, it must always have a seminary trained priest as a mentor. In our twenty-one years of existence we have had five. Our first was the aforementioned Ron Smith from Coaticook. Our current mentor is from the diocese of New Hampshire. The mentor attends all regular team meetings, and duties are varied. In the beginning, our mentor had to teach us from scratch everything about conducting a service that a seminarian would have learned at school, or picked up during internship. Later, at our request, the mentor shifted to offering training in subjects relating to outreach and church growth.

Second, we were to function in teams. It is rare that any one of us will do a service alone. At eucharist there could be three: the celebrant, a preacher, and a lay reader. For morning prayer we will generally have two, a preacher and a lay reader. This makes for inspired scheduling since we are assigning people who also hold full-time jobs.

Third, as a team, we were to undertake courses of study on a continuing basis. This we divided into two parts. That portion of our study that is specifically oriented to the operation or understanding of the Episcopal or Anglican churches, their history and liturgy, is taught by the mentor at regular meetings of the administrative team. Those courses that are biblically oriented, or cover general seminary subjects such as biblical history, literature, and so forth, are taught separately by teachers recruited for that purpose.

Finally, we were to meet at regular intervals. In the early years, this meant about three times a month. Now, depending on our study schedule, we meet generally twice a month.

This team ministry has not only survived, it has flourished. Twenty-four years after commissioning the administrative team, there are five locally ordained priests and one deacon, three licensed lay preachers, and two lay readers providing ministerial coverage for the three churches of the Border Parish.

Two of the three churches are holding their own, though the third, which had earlier almost burnt itself out taking care of the other two, is struggling. (But even there we have hope, as one of its preachers is now going through the process for ordination, and has future growth very much on his mind.) The mission and outreach dimension of parish life is still alive and well. We hope the new generation of priests being identified for local ordination will be able to build on the foundation passed on by those of the older generation. Mission and outreach are very much a part of their future.

Prior to the advent of team ministry, the only thing the three missions were unable to do was provide funds for the salary of a full-time incumbent. This was paid for from the coffers of the three dioceses. The three missions were always and are still able to raise sufficient funds to keep their buildings in good shape and to pay their assessments. In fact, one of the churches has gone through a significant remodelling program, ending up debt free. Apart from the $1,500 US a year for the costs of the administrative team, none of us is paid, though our respective vestries generally reimburse us for expenses we incur on their behalf. The basic concept of "tent-maker ministry" is that each minister of the parish — priest, preacher, lay reader — is expected to have an independent income capable of meeting his or her personal and family needs without having to call on the church for help.

EDUCATING FOR MUTUAL MINISTRY

A Community Based Model
Qu'Appelle

Donald Phillips

During my first year as a parish incumbent, a young man who had recently joined the parish agreed to become a server. He was well motivated and seemed to grasp the training I offered without difficulty. Even though he performed all the tasks of a server with precision, there was something superficial about it: he seemed uneasy and present in the sanctuary only in body. After his second or third turn at serving, he attended a weekend conference where he was given a glimpse of his place among the people of God and how his whole life was an integral part of God's plan for the church and for the world. Being a server was neither directly nor indirectly a part of the weekend's agenda, yet the next time he served, the change in him was remarkable. He carried out the tasks as before, but now he was "present" in the sanctuary and moved around it "like he owned the place." Serving had become for him more than a learned task — it was a legitimate role he assumed in the community.

On the other hand, I have been frustrated and disappointed when someone who has the skills and knowledge to do a job properly or well — being a warden or preaching — withdraws because he or she "didn't feel comfortable" in a leadership role. Somehow, their legitimacy in that role had not been affirmed. We have something important to learn from this about how people receive training and education so that they are truly empowered and involved in ministry.

Educating for Mutual Ministry assumes a dramatic difference in how the church is viewed. The terminology of a two-tiered system of clergy and lay people no longer works. Instead, terms such as "the body of Christ" and "the whole people of God" reveal the foundational principle that every Christian is baptized into ministry in church and in daily life. The goal is not to train people to be church technicians who have a reasonable grasp of, and competency in, various tasks but can only replicate what they've experienced. Rather, it is to equip people to understand the "essence" of their ministry, to interpret the scriptural and theological underpinnings of ministry, and to be proficient and competent in recreating, not just replicating, what they've experienced. We want them to move around in their parish community "like they own the place."

In my experience, this happens most effectively when learning takes place within the community or congregation where ministry is to be practised. This finding is well supported by recent work in educational psychology on *situated learning*, which indicates that learning improves when individuals participate in a community where they can identify the skills that they are acquiring with specific roles. It is a learning model that especially applies to candidates identified by congregations for local ministry.

A challenge then in training people for Mutual Ministry is to ensure that learning happens in the context of a *community of practice*, and that the community correspond as closely as possible to the real communities to which the student belongs. Traditional seminaries may go to great lengths to create a "living community," but these often bear little resemblance to the students' home congregations or to the future congregations in which they will serve. Significantly, many seminaries today place increasing importance on their students' involvement in parish internships and the integration of this experience into their college learning.

Another challenge in delivering education to adult learners is to take account of the time, energy, motivation, and financial resources that learners are able to direct to the program.

The single parent who works full time and is involved in volunteer efforts in the church and community may have limited time and energy for ministry training. It is pointless to challenge such a person to greater commitment. This was our experience when the diocese of Qu'Appelle offered the Education for Ministry program, an extension course developed by the University of the South, which involved weekly meetings and homework for nine months of the year. Even though it is an excellent course, only a very few people could commit themselves to that extent.

In a community based education model, as in traditional university-level program models, the assumption is that learners will grow in theological competency and spiritual maturity. At the same time, they will be expected to be able to help others do the same. Rather than reinforce a separation between personal and church life, or set up a distinction between professional and lay competencies, the challenge is to help learners integrate ministry in church and daily life, including work and school, family and community, and volunteer and paid service.

EDUCATIONAL PROGRAMS

Training programs for Mutual Ministry can be offered either as in-depth training in a subject area for a small number of participants, or as a more generalized overview of a subject area for larger groups. The diocese of Qu'Appelle has developed a two-tiered program. The basic core level program, intended for larger groups, consists of self-contained evening and weekend workshops given by the trainer in the host parish. It is offered in several different locations around the diocese and is open to all, with no requirement for advance preparation. The program for advanced or specialized training, by contrast, is geared towards smaller groups. It is more intensive and requires participants to pre-register, to prepare ahead of time, and sometimes to travel greater distances.

The basic core level program

The core level program is designed to be flexible and to reach as many people as possible. To achieve this, course modules have been developed in a "laddering" system, for use by a variety of learning groups. In the area of worship and liturgy, for example, the same course module is offered to people moving towards ordination, to people planning to lead worship but not be ordained, and to those preparing to coordinate worship but not necessarily lead it. Depending on their situation, individuals might attend one or more workshops on a given subject, or a group might gather for several weeks to work through a written course covering the same material.

Adult learners in non-academic settings generally need to see immediate application for their learning in order to be motivated to go into greater depth. So, for example, instead of beginning with introductory courses in scripture and philosophy, our training programs might begin with workshops about daily ministry that many are already doing, or about the nature and practice of Anglicanism. These are both areas in which learners can readily make the connection between their own experience and the course material.

Our core level curriculum includes introductory workshops in the nature of ministry, Anglicanism, Old and New Testaments, church history, liturgy and worship, initiation, pastoral care, mission in daily life, and congregational dynamics and leadership. Our hope is that people who cover all these areas will have a solid and broad foundation for training in specialized ministry, while others are free to be involved to whatever degree they wish.

Ideally, those who do the training are people who participate in the life and worship of the learners' own congregations. In reality, this ideal is difficult to attain. The important thing is that trainers view the learners as legitimate participants in the learning community, and that workshops and training events convey the feeling of being an authentic dialogue among participants. A trainer must be able to genuinely affirm the contribution of learners. We have tended to invite faculty members from a nearby seminary, particularly in more academic subject areas, and people from the diocese who are theologically educated, as workshop presenters. This gives the sense that trainers and learners are part of the larger "community of practice" that is our diocese. Those trainers who are keenly aware of being learners themselves are the most effective at creating the right kind of learning environment.

Most distance delivery programs are concerned to provide "mentor services," considered advisable on the assumption that long-distance learners need to gather with other learners and a trainer in their area in order to discuss course material and insights. However, we were pleasantly surprised by the growth in several of our training teams without such a resource. We noted that assimilation and integration of the material presented was greatest among those who were active in the particular area of ministry. Learners would naturally discuss subjects that related directly to their ministry role. Thus, while having local mentors is desirable, it may be less critical than we initially thought.

ADVANCED OR SPECIFIC TRAINING

When moving beyond basic training into specialized areas of ministry, the number of participants drops significantly. As the need for role identification by the learner becomes more critical, so does the importance of situated learning. For example, those taking advanced level training in pastoral care need to identify with people who are doing or teaching pastoral care, so that they can also see themselves as valid pastoral-care workers. So, in addition to work-shops and conferences, the learners must work closely with practitioners, and at a level beyond mere observation. Mutuality is important, and learners need to feel that their questions and comments help to enlighten and build upon the understanding and experience of the trainer. Projects and regular interaction with a mentor are important parts of this phase.

ASSESSMENT

While many of us may prefer traditional tools of evaluation, we need to remember that what examinations and written assignments actually assess is a learner's ability to recall and reproduce factual information. However, when it comes to assessing formation and skills in ministry, we are really seeking assurance that a person has developed the abilities and understanding necessary to assume a ministerial role in the community. A learner needs to be able to replicate that role in a way that meets the community's expectations, as well as be able to scrutinize the practice of ministry critically and suggest improvements. In leading worship, for example, one wants assurance that the learner can effectively plan and lead worship in a way that is both continuous with and expands on the community's worship tradition. The best assessment will occur over a period of time from within the community, by members who are able to affirm a person's readiness for the new ministerial role for which he or she is training.

In Qu'Appelle diocese, attendance is taken at basic level workshops. Participants in advanced level training build a learning covenant, keep a learning journal that is shared with a mentor, arrange interviews with practitioners, complete one or more projects, and meet twice with a diocesan ministry assessment team. While these "assignments" may vary, the steps are the same for all of the formally commissioned and ordained ministries. Each parish has some latitude in naming the various ministries for which it is seeking training for individuals. Typically, the list includes worship, pastoral care, education, ecumenical relations, preaching, outreach, administration, stewardship, and becoming a deacon or priest. In small congregations, sometimes two or more of these ministries are combined.

DIOCESAN AND LOCAL NEEDS

A challenge we have faced is the differences in priorities for the diocese and the local community. Whereas the diocese (and the diocesan coordinator) might value uniformity and standardization, the local community may place more importance on its own need for ministry and what the learner needs to fill it. We strive for a balance by structuring the training program as a partnership between the diocese and the parish. The rationale is that, while the diocese is familiar with the resources and expected standards of training for the wider church, the local church is familiar with its members and the ministry needs and opportunities for which training is designed.

In conclusion, perhaps the most important feature of the program we offer is on the job training. Persons who decide to participate in the training do so because they have already identified with the ministry role they are exploring. As adults, they already have a wealth of experience, some of it awaiting reflection and enlightenment, which will continue to inform their understanding and practice of ministry. Our role is to help them discover and participate in learning communities so that they can continue to move forward as legitimate practitioners in ministry.

Urban and Community Ministry

RIVER NORTH ANGLICAN PARISHES

A Story of Cluster Ministry
Rupert's Land

Maylanne Maybee with Peter Flynn

Total or Mutual Ministry is more than a model of congregational life: it's a set of principles, values, and relationships. The church is learning to apply them, not just in situations where a parish can no longer afford a clergy stipend but in a variety of situations that call for an alternative to the one-priest/one-parish model of ministry. Linking parishes together in clusters and forming a ministry team can also work, provided the right conditions are present.

From 1972 to 1987, River North Anglican Parishes in Winnipeg served as a model of clustering and team ministry. And although the social context, which helped it to flourish, has changed considerably over the last twenty-five years, the story still bears relating. For those who took part in its making, telling their story is an occasion to evaluate and bring closure to that experience. For any who have considered clustering, there is much here that is valuable to learn.

. . .

In April 1972, an experiment began that had lasting significance for the parishes in question, for the diocese of Rupert's Land, and for the wider church. Five parishes — St. Anne's, St. Barnabas, St. Catherine, St. Martin-in-the-Field, and St. Paul, Middlechurch

— joined together as a cluster to form River North Anglican Parishes under the pastoral care of a team ministry.

The joyful celebration of an Easter sunrise service marked its beginning. The new clergy team plus members from all the River North parishes participated, as well as the clergy and members of the local United Church congregation. One parishioner recalls, "There was a large attendance in the church and upper hall where a public address system had been set up. As the communion was being administered, the sun rose, shining through the east windows, bringing a feeling of peace and promise of stability after years of change. After the service, breakfast was served in the lower hall, and those present had the opportunity to meet their new clergy and parishioners of River North."

The cluster experiment was initiated by the Rt. Rev. Barry Valentine, the diocesan bishop at the time, after much planning and discussion with parish leaders and clergy. He proposed the structure as a way of sharing resources, giving and receiving mutual support among clergy and people, and deploying ordained leadership across several parishes in a creative and consultative way.

At the time of formation, some parishes were able to contribute financially and others needed assistance. Parish rolls ranged from 40 families or households in one parish to 140 in another, for a total membership of about 450 households or families. Parish income levels ranged from $5,000 (in 1971 dollars) at the low end, to $20,000 at the high end; and a capital debt load ranged between $6,000 in the poorest parish and $42,000 in the largest and fastest growing. A decision was made to establish a central financial structure that would control expenditures for clergy stipends, travel, music, office staff and supplies, and mortgage payments. Individual parishes would be responsible for rectory maintenance, property taxes, and local renovations.

Diocesan canons required each parish to form its own corporation (incumbent plus wardens), and parishes preferred to identify with their own priest. The clergy who gave leadership to the initial cluster included the Ven. Michael Peers, the Rev. Duncan Wallace, and the Rev. Allan Reed. In addition to these clergy on full stipends (one of whom was shared with the diocesan office), two non-stipendiary priests completed the team: the Rev. J.T.L. James, a provincial corrections officer, and the Rev. Michael Hicks, a professor at the University of Manitoba. "It is my hope," said Bishop Valentine, "that in this way our Anglican people will have both a sense of 'their own parish priest' in the neighbourhood and also a share in the skills and gifts of a wider group of men [*sic*]."

The Rev. Canon Peter Flynn, an "alumnus" of River North, recently assembled a group of people who had been active within it cluster to tell their collective story of a successful survival strategy that became much more. Ted and Betty Ash recalled moving into the parish of St. Anne in 1971. When their rector, Archdeacon Ralph Baxter, left several years later for another appointment, they and others in the parish worried whether they could afford another priest. The cluster offered a viable alternative. "We were really impressed with River North. We still kept our own identity — women's groups, servers, youth groups — and our own services. But the cluster meant we could get up to 500 people out for big events. Smaller numbers just couldn't have done the same kind of thing."

As the discussion unfolded and memories quickened, some names came up regularly: Laurie Ward from St. Anne's, George Thomson from St. Martin's, Edna Balderstone from St. Paul's, Harold Biddulf from St. Catherine's, Charlotte Kozi from St. Barnabas's. The energy and constancy of parishioners like these were crucial factors in the success and longevity of River North Anglican Parishes.

People recalled that the first combined social event was a fall corn roast, followed the next year by a summer parish picnic. This marked the beginning of an annual event at which parishioners from cluster churches could meet and socialize. Lenten programs and confirmation classes drew from all five churches and rotated among the sites. Over time a network of cooperation and friendship grew up among the five parishes. The activities were largely family focused: a drama group and choir, a medieval banquet, an annual curling bonspiel known as "The Copper Whisk" (represented by a straw whisk mounted on a plaque and spray painted copper). One year there was an inter-parish Historical Tour and Ascension Day Service, for which each parish prepared a history display and cluster parishioners travelled to each church. The tour ended with a eucharist and refreshments. Parents were able to present their children with a range of team sports and fun events to choose from, and training Sunday school teachers was nowhere near the headache it can be in smaller parishes. Confirmations took place at the cathedral, with not a word of objection because of the unifying quality of a joint occasion.

The cluster was overseen by the River North Council, made up of the clergy and two elected representatives per parish, who ran the general affairs of the cluster, paid salaries and utility bills, and provided major supplies and office support to participating parishes. A central office was established in St. Anne's Church, and a cluster secretary, who helped to coordinate the activities of the five parishes and to publish a quarterly newsletter, was hired. Outreach, mission, education, and finances all came under the River North committee structures.

Having a council made up of both clergy and lay people helped to ensure continuity and maintain the flavour of the cluster, even when there was turnover. Nevertheless, people recalled that scheduling was a challenge, and that meetings were time consuming and could often run late. This could be especially hard on lay leaders, as those who were elected to the River North Council were also expected to serve on a committee. On the plus side, the cluster model allowed for strong committees capable of accomplishing a great deal. Support for each other's functions meant that success bred success.

Certain measures ensured the success and viability of River North Parishes. One of the clergy team was designated priest supervisor of River North, thus building an oversight function into the structure. The clergy selection process included discernment about whether candidates for the cluster would be open to working in a team. Parishes had a direct hand in screening and interviewing candidates. Selection committees, which included representatives from the other parishes in the cluster, would put forward three names to the bishop, who then made the final appointment. In this way, it was possible to balance a parish selection process with the building of an intentional team. As new clergy joined a parish in the cluster, they were warmly welcomed. Wardens would introduce them to each parish, and representatives of the team would participate in each induction service. (The procedure has since changed: now the parish selects from among names preselected by the bishop, giving less latitude for handpicking a cluster team.)

Cluster clergy rotated between parishes once a month, giving parishioners the opportunity to become comfortable with other clergy, and offering them a range of different gifts. Sharing clergy across parishes was also a big plus when it came to covering for holidays, absences, and illnesses. The downside was that every parish event was multiplied times five! Attending a fall fair at St. Anne's also meant attending fall fairs for the parishes of St. Barnabas, St. Catherine, St. Martin, and St. Paul. And it wasn't just the clergy who showed solidarity in this way. River North parishioners shared a sense of mutual obligation to support each other's activities. It was part of the glue that held things together.

At the same time, clustering enhanced local celebrations, and made it possible to be more flexible and experimental in matters of liturgy and ministry. There was much hilarity in recalling five paschal candles at the Easter Vigil, which rotated from one parish to another; or the chore of chaperoning confirmation class overnights; or organizing the annual parish picnic and trying to share "the River North Bus" among five parishes. The cooperative spirit among the parishes helped to ease the process of liturgical reform during the early 1980s, an era that introduced the New Zealand liturgy, the Canadian Rite 4, and eventually the *Book of*

Alternative Services. In 1985, there was agreement to admit baptized children to communion with parental approval and suitable preparation. One of the first Anglican women to be ordained to the priesthood in Canada was brought in as priest-in-charge of St. Catherine's with little resistance or controversy, and by all accounts, with strong support and collegiality from other clergy members of the cluster.

Though conflict and differences existed, everyone involved affirmed their high level of comfort with each other, the absence of hidden agendas or conflicting messages, and the general spirit of warm welcome.

In November 1982, the cluster celebrated its tenth anniversary with a service of rededication in St. John's Cathedral, followed by a dinner in the parish hall of St. Martin's. Special guests at this dinner were priests who had formed the first team, with entertainment from the River North Players.

During the years following the tenth anniversary, however, member parishes started to move in different directions. The River North structure required high energy among the laity, and smaller churches were finding it difficult to get people to serve as lay representatives on the cluster council. St. Anne's and St. Catherine's had shared an incumbent throughout the life of the cluster, but St. Anne's now wanted its own full-time rector. The River North Council struggled long and hard with this decision, but once it was made, it led to others.

St. Catherine's, serving the mushrooming bedroom community of Bird's Hill, had been one of the churches to gain strength through the cluster arrangement. Its history reveals much activity and growth in the 1980s — increased revenues, renovations to the parish hall, the final payment of their mortgage, the beginning of its own parish newsletter. Of the cluster parishes, it had been the one on the edge geographically, requiring extra travel to River North events. In July 1986, after many months of deliberation, the congregation of St. Catherine resolved to withdraw from River North Parishes.

St. Martin's voted next to withdraw. For St. Barnabas's, the breakup was daunting: "We didn't have enough financial resources to make it on our own.... Where would we go to get our resources and people?" In the end, the dissolution of River North Parishes proved to be an incentive to self-sufficiency, and St. Barnabas's was eventually able to make it on its own. Shared secretarial services continued for a while after the breakup on a fee for service basis.

The end came as a result of many factors. When the effort to sustain the cluster became unsupportable, the only option was to take the high ground and bring it to closure. The Ven. Phil Barnett, a clerical member of the cluster, reflected on the dissolution of the partnership.

> The last few months have been very difficult for those of us who have enjoyed the River North association. We have been in a time of limbo — waiting for the end, which we know is coming, and not too sure what it's going to be like afterwards. In many ways it has been like waiting for someone to die. We have tried to carry on with life as best we can, but without a whole lot of energy or enthusiasm. Our thoughts have wandered over all the good times that we had together — the things we accomplished, the joy of making new friends — and also remembered the difficulties and struggles that we went through together. We're sure going to miss all that when it's gone.
>
> After the death, though, there is still life, life in new ways. The parishes will carry on in their new arrangements. The things that we have experienced together in the past will help to shape who we are in the future. We have been privileged to share a life together for a while, and now as we go separate ways we carry with us those experiences, which will hopefully have a positive effect on our approach to ministry.... The legacy of River North will still bear

fruit in the lives of those who are part of it. There is, after all, life after death. Thanks be to God.

There was ambivalence about the way in which the experiment ended. Some reflected that, had there been diocesan commitment to "keep this thing going," things might have turned out differently. Looking back, some felt that reaching out to the community was getting short shrift from the arrangement, that a structure could and should have been developed to support community ministries. Leadership training was mentioned as a missing piece. Others mentioned the tension that existed between the desire for local autonomy and the expectations of being part of a cluster. For example, though it was claimed that supplies would be cheaper if bought in bulk, problems arose when one of the churches started to hoard supplies — the beginning of the end! Some would have preferred an evaluation closer to the time of dissolution. At the time there was no assessment, no autopsy.

Everyone agreed, however, that the cluster left a positive legacy. Both clergy and laity learned strong leadership skills. Some later took strong roles at the diocesan and national levels, and carried forward an interest in and commitment to global issues. One lay leader became chair of the Primate's World Relief and Development Fund Committee through his involvement with River North. The list of clergy who served in River North Anglican Parishes now reads like a roll call of bishops, archdeacons, and deans. The precedent of working in a team led to another arrangement in which the dean and three archdeacons also worked in a team relationship with the bishop. Participating parishes have subsequently assumed a stronger outward focus, with greater potential and willingness among the laity to volunteer at the diocesan level. Participants affirmed that River North was a successful survival move with outcomes beyond initial expectations. It accomplished all its goals.

What made River North Anglican Parishes work when some other similar experiments have not?

1. *The parishes entered the cluster from a position of relative demographic strength.* The participating churches of River North, though struggling, were not in serious decline, and some were even entering into a period of growth.

2. *The bishop gave leadership and unqualified support.* River North was initiated by the bishop in consultation with its member parishes. There was some "bottom up" consent, and a concerted effort to ensure "buy in" by participating churches. But the drive and commitment to create the cluster was given crucial impetus at the diocesan level, and continued to be supported by the way in which clergy were selected and appointed.

3. *Age and sociological composition of participating parishes were fairly similar.* River North Parishes sponsored community and family activities — sports, dinners, drama, youth events, and celebrations — all of which benefited from strength in numbers. Parishioners enjoyed cultural compatability and mutual interests.

4. *The cluster was not driven by an immediate need to close parishes or sell property.* There was a certain genius in the River North arrangement, whereby each participating parish retained a sense of having its own priest, and each had autonomy over its own property. The River North cluster offered a synergy of being more than the sum of its parts.

5. *Perhaps the most critical factor in making the cluster work was the spirit of those who participated.* There was a refreshing sense of fun, enthusiasm, and mutual regard, which no amount of strategic planning or organizational structure could have replaced. I asked what people had learned from their experiment in ministry, and what they might have done differently. "We challenged each other to be on our best behaviour," was one comment. "The last thing we ever cut from our budgets was our diocesan commitment."

Opinions differed about the decision to disband. Those whom I met said the decision was not regretted. Other sources suggested that the end was "the culmination of a long and often agonized process as the many efforts to heal the divisions in River North were unsuccessful." Yet it seems to have been "a good death" — there was celebration, mourning, and energy to carry on in new ways.

In many ways, the ability to discern the moment when it needed to end was one of the strengths of the cluster. Throughout its fourteen years, the River North Council had checked annually to decide whether and how the cluster would continue. One of the smaller parishes at the outset became one of the bigger ones at the end. At the time of dissolution, three mortgages were entirely paid off. There was more confidence in the parishes about their future. Looking back over the mists of time, former participants agreed that, for the time it existed, the cluster was a lifesaver. There was even a hint about the possibility of trying again.

THE INDUSTRIAL CAPE BRETON EXPERIMENT

Regional Ministry Development
Nova Scotia and Prince Edward Island

Jack Risk

Against the background of the shift to a post-industrial economy currently taking place in Cape Breton, Nova Scotia, an exciting experiment is underway in regional ministry development. Recently amalgamated into a single municipality, the territory from Sydney Mines on the northwest to Louisbourg on the east — encompassing North Sydney, Coxheath, and Sydney River, the city of Sydney (along with Whitney Pier), and coastal towns such as New Waterford, Dominion, Glace Bay, and Port Morien — constitutes the second largest concentration of population in the province. This is the land where steel, coal, and fish supported thriving communities for generations. Within the last decade all this has changed. Churches in the region have found themselves confronted by a situation in which the given pattern of life can no longer be taken for granted.

Over the last three years the nine Anglican parishes in the region comprising seventeen congregations have been working towards the discernment of a common sense of mission. The diversity of the churches of the region is notable. There are rural, small town, and city parishes. One can find multi-congregation parishes, satellite congregations, and large single-congregation parishes. Some congregations are isolated by distance while Sydney has an oversupply of church buildings. In some cases, financial viability and declining membership are presenting congregations with hard decisions. In others, the congregation needs to come to terms with its long-range sense of mission and relevance to its environment.

Alongside all this diversity is the startling reality that the seventeen congregations in Industrial Cape Breton all lie within a radius of less than an hour's drive. This fact, together with the strong cultural cohesiveness of the region, point to an impressive potential for regionalized ministry and mission.

As diocesan program officer, I began working with these parishes in the fall of 1998. A recently completed task force report led to the formation of a Core Group of two lay and one clergy member from each congregation. It was clear there was substantial energy for change. There were pressures motivating it from within the churches: concern for church tradition and future ministry coupled with the ageing and declining membership, declining income and increased costs, and the difficulty of attracting and paying for full-time clergy. Moreover, conflicts and divisions pointed to a loss of vision and an inability to respond to current needs. Other pressures motivating change came from without: economic depression, depopulation and the departure of the young, the short supply of clergy, and cultural changes characteristic of modern secular Canada.

The Core Group was determined to enter into a multi-year project dedicated to inducing the congregations to participate in a process of far-ranging modernization. In the two and a half years since it began, considerable numbers of parishioners have joined in the process. All worked on the clearly understood assumptions that there were no-predetermined outcomes, no diocesan expectations were laid on, and all changes and developments were to take place by consensus. My role was to facilitate highly participatory and open-ended discussion.

Beginning in the spring of 1999 and continuing for most of a year, members of the Core Group discussed and conducted research into various aspects of the organizational lives of the parishes. The first aim of the research was to equip the parishes with a realistic understanding of their current situations. Sharing parish information publicly could serve to break down the sense of parochial isolation and build a sense of trust and shared vulnerability. It would also help identify issues and problems that could better be dealt with by approaching issues of ministry and mission on a regional basis.

The Core Group divided itself into three working groups to undertake the collecting and initial analysis of data.

Mission

The Mission Working Group assembled a list of more than thirty organizations, agencies, and individuals in the Industrial Cape Breton region whom they felt would be able to inform the Core Group of the character of the community and the issues confronting it. A series of interviews was organized to be undertaken by members of the congregations. Over twenty people assisted with this work.

A protocol of questions was devised to assist the volunteers in conducting their interviews, and an orientation workshop was conducted for interviewers by the chair of the working group. Several types of information were being sought: the needs and strengths of the community, the purpose and needs of the particular organization being interviewed, perceptions of church involvement in the community, the potential for forming partnerships and coalitions with others in the community.

A series of five workshops was conducted to draw useful information out of the stories the volunteers had brought back with them from their community interviews. Participants in the workshops identified possibilities for new regional Anglican projects that might serve the community and would also reflect the congregations' Anglican identity. One clear message brought back from many of the interviews was that community agencies were not receiving needed help from the churches. The result was a list of over sixty concrete possibilities for new regional cooperation in outreach to the wider community.

NUMBERS

The Numbers Working Group gathered statistics from the annual reports of the congregations and assembled these into graphs. Donated income and expenses, together with average Sunday attendance and membership figures, were charted over a six-year period to reveal any trends.

Along with graphs of individual congregations' statistics, a summary table was assembled, comparing finances and membership for the region. Several findings emerged from this tabulation. Attendance, membership, and number of donors were flat or declining in most parishes. Rising costs and decreasing membership had led to an ever-increasing burden on individual givers. These graphs showed how financial security in most parishes was dependent on people in their sixties, seventies, or higher.

RESOURCES

Most of the discussions of the Resources Working Group hovered around the questions: What is the best configuration of assets to support ministry over the long term? and, Is there a sustainable strategy for the organization of ministry? Doubts were raised about the ability of congregations to maintain the current number of church buildings. Some parishes were experiencing difficulty in hiring. Two of the parishes had undertaken commitments to Non-Stipendiary Ordained Ministry (NSOM). Ideas on a variety of forms of team ministry came forward.

Ultimately, an all-day workshop, at which the Resources Working Group was assisted by a further dozen parishioners, roughed out some tentative proposals for realignments and team ministries. Three subregions within Industrial Cape Breton, each to be served by a team of lay and ordained persons, were contemplated as a way of sharing resources within localities. Various short-term suggestions were put forward as means towards building cooperation and breaking down parish isolation.

The Resources Working Group also assembled detailed maps of the region, and plotted every Anglican household on them. Parishes were requested to complete a questionnaire on physical assets, and an inventory has been compiled from the responses received.

RESPONSE FROM THE PARISHES

The findings and suggestions of the three working groups were presented in May 2000. The meeting, to which all the Parish Councils and Regional Council members were invited, was attended by over one hundred and sixty persons — the largest meeting in the history of the region. The Core Group invited the parishes to take part in serious regional discussions of the possibilities for a shared future. The Core Group strongly insisted that all suggestions made in its report were to be taken only as starting points for discussion and as examples of creative solutions to regional issues.

Overt reactions to the May presentation were more positive than the Core Group had anticipated. The fact, however, that their suggestions for discussion had included the possible reduced use or closing of several churches was bound to generate anxiety, if not opposition.

Parish Discussion Process

It was clear that the parishes needed to begin their own discussions as a step towards coming on board. I prepared a curriculum to guide discussions within parishes, which became known as the Parish Discussion Process. Along with other topics, the content of the course dealt with: the history of the congregation, the life-cycle of congregations, the experience of change, the situation of the Industrial Cape Breton parishes, participants' visions for the future, different dimensions to church growth, baptismal ministry, and opportunities for regional cooperation.

The format was an adult education program in three sessions. The third session was to be held in conjunction with a neighbouring congregation. Fifteen of the co-leaders trained within the region under the diocesan Logos program were recruited, and these were assisted by several other volunteer facilitators. The co-facilitators were given training in the materials.

Approximately half the parishes completed the parish discussion process as intended. In a few cases, more recent progress has been reported. Where the course was completed, the ultimate reception was generally positive. In one instance, strong resistance was voiced as a result of the perception that the project was seeking to impose church closures.

An interesting development during the course of the parish discussion process was that two of the parishes, Whitney Pier and New Waterford-Dominion, entered into a new yoking relationship. While our project was credited with having made this new arrangement possible, Core Group members from these parishes were adamant that the sharing of a clergy person's salary was not a long-term solution.

In general, the perception was emerging among the Core Group that the project ought to move towards initiating concrete cooperative activities and promoting inter-parish discussions.

A week-long series of events was put together for March 2001. These were designed to remotivate participation, encourage creative thinking around the options for regionalized ministry, and clarify the future direction of the project.

The help of two American resource persons with experience of clustering experiments and regionalized ministries was engaged. A day-long workshop on models of ministry was attended by over seventy-five persons. Materials were introduced to support small group worship and Bible reflection. Themes of presentations included the baptismal covenant, existing experiments in parish clustering, and principles of regional ministry. A presentation on Mutual Ministry was made by members of the diocese who had taken part in tours of the diocese of Northern Michigan. A member of the Core Group who had been a delegate to the 2001 Annual Conference of Living Stones spoke of how the Industrial Cape Breton project had been reported on and discussed in the context of other experiments in Total Ministry. Workshops were devoted to clustering of congregations, covenanting for discernment, and evaluating options for outreach projects. A regional eucharistic liturgy following the Saturday workshop was attended by over two hundred persons.

By the time the March Events had concluded, substantial progress had been made on several fronts. A meeting was held several days later to which the parish councils and other interested parishioners were invited. Over seventy persons attended. At that meeting, the legitimacy of the Core Group was confirmed. Core Group members expressed a sense of being re-energized. There was general enthusiasm among non-Core Group participants and a renewed commitment to the objectives of the project. Clarifying the broad objectives of the project went some distance toward calming the anxieties that had been generated in some quarters about the purpose of the project being to close churches. The value of small congregations was affirmed, along with an understanding of how the ministry of small congregations can be supported within a regional ministry strategy. Regional ministry emerged as a workable strategy for organizing resources to meet the congregations' mandates for mission and ministry. Baptismal ministry was clearly named as not only the focal theological motif but also a workable strategy on which to build local ministry.

PRINCIPLES FOR DEVELOPING REGIONAL MINISTRY

During the winter of 2001 including the March Events, we developed a list of principles that will guide the growth of regional ministry in Industrial Cape Breton. Jesus and the gospel will be at the centre of whatever we do together. Inwardly we will focus on learning to be disciples. Outwardly we will focus on our mission as apostles. Each baptized Christian has a ministry. In building shared mission and ministry, our goal is the increased ministry of each congregation, not mere survival.

The door is open for each congregation to participate in regional ministry as it sees fit. All are equal partners. Local problems require local solutions. Structures will be loose and flexible to permit growth and movement. The diocese is a partner in regional ministry — a servant rather than a master. Each congregation will make its own decisions about its own future. Congregations will support each other's decisions and promote the independence and self-reliance of each. There will be no forced closures and no rescues or artificial life support.

The process is open-ended. Goals may differ, but we will arrive at them together. We will listen carefully to each other. Congregations will support each other's aspirations and liturgical traditions. We will keep talking for as long as it takes until we know what God is calling us to do together.

Looking ahead

The culmination of the March Events was the establishment of three new working groups to consider ways of putting the principles into practice. One, focusing on vision and dialogue, will meet with individual parishes and design a process of discerning options for the future of the region. Another will design and implement regional outreach projects and programs. The third will make sure that everybody is kept informed of developments.

In May 2001, diocesan synod received a presentation on regional ministry development as a potential strategy for developing the diocese as a whole. At the presentation, my new book, *Regional Ministry Development: An Invitation to Dialogue*, was launched. It contains a report on the Industrial Cape Breton experiment, a primer on congregational development, a manual for regional projects, and a set of proposals for a diocesan strategy of regional ministry development. If the churches of Industrial Cape Breton are able to pioneer some cooperative strategies, they will be in a position to serve the entire diocese as a laboratory of innovation in ministry. While the Industrial Cape Breton project has been moving forward, other complementary initiatives have been taking place in the wider diocese. A well-developed Non-Stipendiary Ordained Ministry program has become established throughout the diocese. Recently a program in the vocational diaconate has been established.

Key diocesan committees have been engaged in the enterprise of promoting diocesan dialogue on these issues. It will take time and much discussion throughout the diocese to develop the necessary overall strategy. Meanwhile we look to the congregations of Industrial Cape Breton to lead us forward.

From Charity to Justice

An Evolving Model of
Community Ministries
Ottawa

Pat Connolly, Sue Garvey

He has showed you, O man, what is good; and what does the Lord require of you but to do justice, and to love kindness, and to walk humbly with your God? (Micah 6:8).

Justice succeeds charity as the principle that guides Christian help to the poor

This God with whom we walk humbly is the God of justice who empowers us to act justly, and the God of love who desires us to love tenderly.

Christians have been reaching out to the poor for centuries — spurred on by scriptures such as, "Whatsoever you do to the least of my people, that you do unto me" (Matthew 25:4, RSV). Paul in one of his letters to the Corinthians says, "And if I give all I possess to the poor ... but have not love, I gain nothing" (1 Corinthians 13:3, NIV). "Love" and "charity" are different New Testament translations for the Greek word *agape*, but in modern usage love is never as cold as charity. The distinction in meaning has arisen because, in their response to the poor over the centuries, the "charity" of church and state has often lost the "love" component.

In England throughout the Middle Ages, the poor went to the monasteries for help, but after the suppression of the monasteries, the government brought in the Elizabethan Poor Law, which formalized charity by making each parish responsible for its own poor. That law remained in place until the 1830s, when a new Poor Law established workhouses of deplorable condition in order to discourage people from relying on "charity." A stern Calvinistic school of thought at the time taught that poverty was a person's own fault. Later, Charles Kingsley initiated a philosophy of "Christian socialism," in which the poor were not blamed for their condition but were regarded as victims of society. This was more in line with the teachings of social justice in both the New and the Old Testament, especially the books of Isaiah, Amos, Hosea, Micah, and the Psalms.[1]

When the Great Depression struck Canada in 1929, government policy at first continued to reflect the old Calvinist ethic, and concerned itself with balancing the budget rather than feeding the hungry. During this time, one Canadian in five was a public dependant. The average yearly income was less than $500, while the poverty line for a family of four was estimated to be more than twice that amount. Yet the Calvinist school of thought so shamed poor people that, even though they were entitled to relief, many couldn't bring themselves to apply for it.[2]

The founding convention of the Co-operative Commonwealth Federation (CCF) in Calgary was of great significance to the transition from a charity model to a justice model in Canada. The

---

1 Philip L. Martin, Member, Ottawa Meeting, Canadian Society of Friends, 1998.
2 Pierre Berton, *The Great Depression* (Toronto: McClelland and Stewart, 1990).

convention's purpose was to form a federation to work for a socialist Canada. The human symbol of the movement, the incorruptible J.S. Woodsworth, was one of the greatest social justice leaders in Canadian history. His doctrine was the Social Gospel. His personal credo may be summed up in his own words: "A curse still hangs over inactivity. A severe condemnation still rests upon indifference.... Christianity stands for social righteousness as well as personal righteousness.... We have tried to provide for the poor. Yet, have we tried to alter the social conditions that lead to poverty?" Woodsworth was a beacon of hope to many who were otherwise hopeless. In those despairing years, he was the conscience of Canada.

In our own times, we have been pondering the distinction between charity and justice. For Christians, this distinction lies at the heart of faith. Fred Kammer, S.J., who has spent years researching the connection between the Judaeo-Christian belief in Yahweh and preferential love for the poor, insists that faith cannot be separated from justice. He believes that the Judaeo-Christian tradition is best served by combining the two concepts into the single word "faithjustice," and promotes the virtue already vibrant in so many people in these terms:

> Faithjustice is a passionate virtue which disposes citizens to become involved in the greater and lesser societies around themselves in order to create communities where human dignity is protected and enhanced, the gifts of creation are shared for the greatest good of all, and the poor are cared for with respect and a special love.[3]

---

3   Fred Kammer, S.J., *Salted With Fire: Spirituality for the Faithjustice Journey* (Mahwah, New Jersey: Paulist Press, 1995).

The Community Ministries
of the Anglican Diocese of Ottawa
OFFER CARE AND ADVOCATE JUSTICE

Throughout the world, faith communities have together established networks of projects and agencies to serve the needs of some of the most vulnerable people in the wider community. The Community Ministries of the Anglican Diocese of Ottawa is one such network. It is a community of ministries that has evolved from *charity provider* to *social justice catalyst*. In our faith justice journey, we recognize that serving justice means concentrating simultaneously on fostering individual change, group and community commitment, and systemic action.

The effectiveness of our community ministries for social justice has been recognized by Mary Hugessen: "The programs which are in place in the Diocese of Ottawa for caring for the poor and disadvantaged are arguably the most sophisticated, comprehensive and well administered of any diocese in Canada."[4] Our community of ministries is made up of four programs:

1. *Centre 454/Anglican Social Services* is a day program providing emotional, spiritual, and practical support to all in need, including those who are homeless, street-involved, or socially isolated. Centre 454 offers counselling, education, advocacy, referral, crisis intervention, and social and recreational activities.

2. *Cornerstone/Le Pilier* offers emergency shelter for homeless women and long-term supportive housing for women rebuilding

---

4   Mary K. Hugessen, "Anglicanism in the Ottawa Valley," in *The Business of the Great King: The Call to Care*, edited by Frank A. Peake (Ottawa: Carleton University Press, 1997).

their lives. Two locations, open twenty-four hours a day, offer professional and practical assistance in a supportive environment.

3. *The Well/La Source* is a day program for women and their children that offers a sense of community with other women. It provides practical, personal, spiritual support, and a light breakfast and full course lunch. It also offers social, recreational, and educational programs, crisis intervention, community information, and group support.

4. *The Ottawa Pastoral Counselling Centre* (OPC) provides counselling of many kinds: individual, marital, family, separation and divorce, depression, grief, sexual orientation, personal crisis, and so on. It is a community based service rooted in Christian beliefs and values, and is open to any person in need.

With the exception of OPC, which serves the broader community, these programs serve people who live in poverty. We see all the attendant miseries that poverty brings: bad housing or none at all, disease, malnutrition, inferior education, and most importantly, general lack of the means to realize one's full potential. Many of those who come to us are "street people" who live by night in our shelters and by day on the streets or in our centres, where we can at least offer them the basics of food, clothing, and shelter from the elements.

Our work is not unique, but we do not always fit into the traditional charity model because we believe that the charity model supports a distinction between the worthy and the unworthy poor, and a distinction in power between the giver and the receiver of charity. Take for example the donation that came to one of our agencies from a local donut shop. Yesterday's donuts arrived in a green garbage bag, many crushed, broken, and stuck together, thus vividly exemplifying the popular principle that "beggars can't be choosers." We called the donor, thanked him, and suggested that future donations to our program be presented as they would be to paying customers. The act of giving should not resemble the "benevolence" of Victorian times but should be an attempt to redistribute the wealth, so that together we are a little more like a true "community."

WE SUPPORT EACH INDIVIDUAL'S DIGNITY AND ENSURE MUTUALITY IN DECISION MAKING

Our Christian faith requires us to support the dignity and self-worth of all people — seeing their strengths and not their weaknesses, recognizing their gifts rather than focusing on their poverty. We strive in a variety of ways to help the people who come to our programs reclaim their personal power. We are careful about the language in program descriptions, attempting to remove words, such as "client," that are suggestive of power differentials. We try to ensure that control is in the hands of the person seeking the support. Our role is to facilitate people's access to the information and resources they need to make the best decisions for their own lives and those of their children. This requires the time needed to build relationships of trust, and the courage to consider and support decisions that would not be our own.

Most importantly, we work with the principle of mutuality, recognizing the benefit derived by all parties in every interpersonal transaction. For example, membership on each of the ministry program committees includes program participants. When the Women in Crisis ministry decided to change its name, the residents of both its housing units were invited to submit their ideas for suitable names, then were invited to participate in an elimination process until all agreed on the name, "Cornerstone/Le Pilier." When Centre 454 faced the monumental task of moving from a location they had occupied for twenty-four years, participants helped search for a new location, joined in the design and renovations, and helped with the actual move. At The Well/La Source, women participate in all levels of programming, including fundraising events that are planned, prepared, and undertaken by participants. At a meeting of The Women of The Well, the disbursement of the funds from these events is decided. Traditionally, some money goes to programming a special event that would otherwise be unaffordable. The women then decide on an amount to donate to another organization, most often in a developing country.

These examples show some ways in which we try to build community with those we serve. A key operating principle for each of the Community Ministries is our goal of establishing a sense of community or belonging among those who use our services. We encourage the development of networks of support, friendship, and solidarity to combat the common experience of isolation and "invisibility," and to act as an alternative source of the help that might otherwise come through family and workplace. Often people who have come to our centres or shelters for particular help develop long-term relationships with each other, and even find accommodation together.

WE SEEK PARTNERS IN OUR WORK WITH THE POOR AND ADVOCACY FOR THE POOR

In addition, our ministries are increasingly finding ways of partnering to stretch and share our resources, and to provide activities that benefit the users of all our agencies. On a community wide basis, we work with a variety of other non-profit government and private partners to accomplish mutual goals. Recently, we have shared facilities with other groups, partnered with a Baptist church to build a new home for women, and received in-kind donations from several businesses to furnish and renovate new buildings to better serve our participants. We have taken key leadership roles in a local lobby group called The Alliance to End Homelessness, maintain strong ties with the National Housing and Homelessness Network, and have participated in the social justice activities of the interfaith coalition Faith Partners.

Our current efforts in this area include the production of a community education package entitled "Choose Hope: A Toolbox for Understanding and Fighting Homelessness in Canada." Co-sponsored by the national Anglican Church, the Community Ministries of the Anglican Diocese of Ottawa, and the Region of Ottawa-Carleton, this package includes a video and a number of educational/ interactive resources to help church and community groups to connect with homelessness and identify ways they can be involved in solving the problem.

OUR ORGANIZATION BALANCES PRACTICAL SUPPORT WITH POLITICAL ADVOCACY FOR A JUST SOCIETY

The directors of the Community Ministries wear many hats. In addition to providing direction and leadership to our individual programs, we advocate for individuals and for the poor in general; we build partnerships with other community groups, striving to improve conditions and working together towards change; and we foster community awareness by facilitating workshops and developing resources such as the multi-media education package. We also work with the participants to ensure that programs are modified to accommodate emerging community needs. As people who provide leadership to agencies that serve the most vulnerable, we are often called upon to speak to groups about homelessness.

These opportunities force us to look beyond our immediate goals of providing compassionate and useful service, to our other responsibility — our prophetic role — as we challenge church and society to promote justice by changing the systems and conditions that produce poverty and homelessness and that keep people marginalized. Therefore, we sit on committees, maintain strong relationships with politicians at all levels, speak to the media and community groups, attend demonstrations, and collaborate in a multitude of partnerships to increase understanding of the urgent need for action on poverty and homelessness in our city and across the country.

A strong Community Ministries board monitors progress, offers program input and policy direction, and participates in evaluation of the services provided by each ministry. The board includes people with relevant expertise who are also involved in the work of at least one of the ministries. Most are members of Anglican parishes; all show faith based commitment to social justice. By their practical involvement in different aspects of the ministries, board members also act as valued sources of personal and professional support and advice to staff members, especially the directors.

The office of the diocese of Ottawa is involved in centralized administration and financial management, in partnership and advocacy with government at all levels, in allocation of synod apportionment monies, and in active support of the work of the Community Ministries with local parishes and the community at large. In tight times, the sound management and support of the diocese have allowed Community Ministries to continue to function despite formidable financial and political challenges.

There are times when the faithjustice values of Community Ministries come into conflict with the priorities of some of our partners, funders, and colleagues, but the diocese and the Community Ministries board have supported us in our holding firmly to our values. For example, recently enacted provincial government legislation that requires social assistance recipients to work for welfare is based on assumptions and principles that are contradictory to ours. For this reason, we have developed a "Policy Statement about Workfare," which explains our refusal to participate in the program despite strong political pressure to do so.

Funding for services to the poorest of the poor has historically been insecure and subject to the ideological stance of the government in power. In addition, there has been in some quarters the view that church based services are offered by people who understand their work as vocation or a God-given call to ministry, and therefore may not have the same moral claim to fair working conditions as other members of the workforce. On the contrary, we believe that workers struggling with the many challenges our participants bring to our doors have the right to excellent service from well-trained and competent professionals, who are not themselves made vulnerable to the risks associated with poor working conditions. The Community Ministries board has established a strong personnel committee whose role it is to develop fair employment standards and practices on behalf of its employees. Despite significant funding constraints, the Community Ministries board is committed to ensuring that its own employment practices are consistent with the principles of justice it promotes in the community.

As a community of God's stewards, we are challenged to walk the faithjustice journey, working towards solidarity and mutuality with the poor. Our stance must be one of prophecy, the ever-uncomfortable role that calls people back to covenant with one another, to shared stewardship of the earth's resources, and to community.

TRADITION AND TRANSFORMATION
The Ministry of St. James'
Vancouver

Michael Batten

A few weeks before Christmas 1960, the angel of the Lord was sent by God to the desk of a library worker at the University of British Columbia. By the end of the day, May Gutteridge had handed in her notice in order to respond to the call to serve the poor. With no clear idea of where to go or how to begin, she was advised by a colleague to make herself known to the priests of St. James' Church, Vancouver's oldest Anglican parish and a flagship of Anglo-Catholic practice and devotion, located in the city's Downtown Eastside.

At first, no one knew what to do with Mrs. Gutteridge. After a visit with the rector of St. James', she was told that there was no particular need at present for her services. But a few weeks later, following one of the mid-week masses, the rector took her aside and suggested that, after all, there was something she could do. The Pensioners' Club, begun a few years earlier as an outreach to the 1,400 pensioners in the community, had lately fallen into the hands of an individual with no connection to the parish, who was now soliciting funds from all over North America in the name of the church. Could she take the matter in hand? "And that," says May, "was how it all began." Before long she was approached by one of the other priests on staff. He was administering the funds of perhaps half a dozen people in the community who had chronic difficulty managing their money. Would May be able to take over the accounts? St. James Social Service Society (now St. James Community Service Society) thus grew piecemeal, responding as best it could to whatever needs were brought to its attention. Using the facilities and name of St. James' parish, it promoted the interests and welfare of those living in the neighbourhood still known as "Canada's poorest postal code."

Vancouver's Downtown Eastside is the oldest part of the city, and includes the popular tourist attractions of Gastown and Chinatown. It is also home to over 16,000 people. The median annual income for males (and 63 per cent of the population is male) in the Downtown Eastside is $9,458. Fully 68 per cent of the people in the Downtown Eastside are classified as "low income," although in some neighbourhoods that figure goes as high as 83 per cent. The overwhelming majority of residents rent accommodation, yet the number of "SROs" (single room occupancy hotels) — the cheapest rental accommodation available — declines year by year. The income assistance caseload in the offices serving the Downtown Eastside area increased by 4 per cent between 1997 and 1998 — to 9,158 — while the total caseload across Vancouver dropped by 13 per cent.

Under such conditions, crime and disease flourish. With 3 per cent of Vancouver's population, the Downtown Eastside accounts for 31 per cent of the city's homicides, 19 per cent of other violent crimes, 11 per cent of thefts from cars, and no less than 74 per cent of all the city's drug arrests. Addiction, whether to drugs or alcohol, is the area's principal health problem. The Vancouver/ Richmond Health Board has identified the three leading causes of death in the Downtown Eastside as alcohol related, AIDS, and drug related, in that order. Men in the Downtown Eastside are nearly three times as likely to die of alcohol related causes as are men in other parts of the city. The health board has declared an AIDS epidemic in the Downtown Eastside, and there are very high incidences of hepatitis, tuberculosis, and syphilis in the community. The area also has a disproportionately high rate of mental illness, with 18 per cent of the city's mental health caseload. Homelessness, poverty, addiction, and illness all shorten life expectancy in the Downtown Eastside, to the extent that a "senior citizen" is anyone over the age of forty-five.

What the grim statistics and lurid news reports fail to convey, however, are the strengths of the Downtown Eastside — strengths that many neighbourhoods and communities in Canada can only wish for. The Downtown Eastside is above all a home and a neighbourhood. To sit in Oppenheimer Park on a summer afternoon is to experience the vitality and diversity of one of the city's most culturally and ethnically varied districts. The residents frequently display a fierce independence, stubbornness, and resourcefulness — qualities often reflected in the work of the Downtown Eastside Residents' Association, one of Canada's most politically active community associations. Because so many of the people in the neighbourhood have experienced profound suffering in their own lives, there is a high level of tolerance, acceptance, and openness towards others. Those who accept the neighbourhood are accepted by it, and the neighbourhood's scorn is generally reserved for those who try to help without getting to know the people or the community. Solutions to the community's problems need to be generated by the community, not imposed from outside. Those who want to help are expected to listen first, to learn what the needs are, and what resources are already available in the community.

The programs of St. James Community Service Society have evolved in response to the changing needs of the Downtown Eastside. May Gutteridge's original half dozen financial administration cases have now grown to over eight hundred and fifty. The society has a large home support program that serves over six hundred clients. It operates an emergency shelter and transitional housing for women and children at risk. It has responded to the chronic housing shortage with a multi-tiered housing program for adults with mental illness, and with residential programs for hard to house adults and at-risk youth. It pioneered the development of free-standing residential hospices in Canada, and through its hospice program provides terminally ill adults with a supportive, comfortable, and caring environment in a warm homelike setting. It also operates a neighbourhood thrift store and a low cost moving service for residents of the Downtown Eastside.

By 1998, St. James Community Service Society had two hundred and fifty-four employees and its annual budget exceeded $7 million. Since most of the society's budget was by now funded from sources other than the parish, the continuing relationship between St. James' parish and the society began to be questioned in some quarters. Was there any need for the society to continue its connection with the church that had brought it to birth? Could the parish continue to offer any meaningful support?

Eventually, both the parish and St. James Community Service Society decided that the church connection needed to be maintained. More was at stake than funding. The needs and concerns of the inner city — alienation, addiction, and abandonment — are symptoms of a deeper spiritual crisis and hunger. That spiritual dimension had long been acknowledged in the society's mission statement, which declares that "it is our intention, in the spirit of Jesus Christ, to offer our service with compassion for each individual and with a concern for social justice, assuring that no person shall be discriminated against for whatever reason." The church connection could help give that declaration a more practical expression. In 1999, the parish and the society decided jointly to fund a chaplaincy, staffed by a priest attached to the parish but completely free of parish responsibilities and able to work full time with the staff, clients, and volunteers of St. James Community Service Society. Although chaplaincies are common in many institutional settings, such a position is something of an innovation in the community service sector.

I was appointed to this new position in September 1999. At first I was a little apprehensive about taking on this work. All my previous experience had been in parish ministry, and I had little interest in traditional forms of chaplaincy. What had originally attracted me to priestly ministry was preaching and the presidency of the liturgy, two roles that do not usually play a large part in a chaplain's work. On the other hand, this was an opportunity to develop a new kind of chaplaincy — and this one would be different from the start: grounded in the liturgical life of the parish, with opportunity both to preach and to celebrate mass regularly.

This liturgical involvement is not a refuge from the challenges of the work; rather, it is the source from which all the work flows. The eucharistic liturgy effects a twofold transformation: as the Holy Spirit transforms the bread and wine into the body and blood of Christ, the church is also transformed through this sacrament into the body of Christ, to carry out the work of Christ in the world. Every eucharistic celebration serves to renew our baptism, whereby we were made members of Christ. Through our participation in the liturgy we are recalled to, and equipped for, Christ's work. The liturgy therefore poses the fundamental challenge that motivates every part of the mission and ministry of the church: Will we allow ourselves to become what we behold and receive? At the same time, the sacramental presence of Christ on the altar challenges us to remember his words: "Whatever you do for the least of my brothers and sisters, you do also for me." The reverence that we show towards Christ in the Blessed Sacrament must also be shown towards Christ's brothers and sisters on the street. This essential connection between our sacramental worship and our ministry in the world requires that every day begins with prayer and worship in the parish church; the work of the church literally begins at the altar as the office is prayed and the eucharist is celebrated. St. James' strong liturgical tradition provides focus, direction, and meaning for my work.

Beyond that, my duties as chaplain are as varied as the society's programs. My primary pastoral involvement is with the hospice program. This involvement is not limited to the residents but also includes their families, the staff, and the many volunteers at the two hospices run by the society. Many of the residents find that their quality of life improves when they move into hospice, with clean and safe accommodations, three square meals a day, and nursing care around the clock. Occasionally, their condition stabilizes and they are able to move back into the community. The average stay, however, is forty-five days. During that time, the goal of the hospice is to provide medical, social, and spiritual support to enable each resident to live as fully and as comfortably as possible, and to help them prepare for death. My role as chaplain in that setting is to help people identify and use their own spiritual resources and traditions to meet their spiritual needs. This is accomplished by listening, grieving, and celebrating with residents; by finding someone of a particular religious tradition to talk or pray with a resident; or by providing opportunity for worship and ritual as required. In addition, I work with hospice staff to provide care for friends and family by participating in events such as the regular memorial services for those who have died in hospice, and the annual Christmas celebration of life. To help address the concerns of those who have been damaged and disempowered by their contact with religious institutions, a brochure on spiritual care, which is given to all residents on admission, also includes a list of the things the chaplain won't do:

- "preach" to you
- try to "save" you
- judge or condemn your lifestyle
- judge or condemn your religious beliefs as wrong or inadequate
- make you join in a particular ritual or accept a particular doctrine

Another focus of pastoral care is the society's residential mental health program, which provides stable long-term housing for seventy-seven people who live with serious mental illness, primarily schizophrenia. One of the devastating consequences of schizophrenia is overwhelming loneliness and social isolation. Helping to overcome this loneliness, as well as encouraging the development of the most basic of daily living skills, is a large part of the care of such persons. This is often made more difficult by the generally short attention span of people with such a condition. One program that is proving popular with this population is something we have called "faith journeys," which brings residents together for half an hour at a time to reflect on the spiritual value of everyday objects and experiences. The conversations are lively, and frequently reveal bright and active minds that are otherwise hidden behind the cloud of mental illness.

A third form of pastoral involvement is an emergency assistance program for those who do not qualify for assistance from any other source or agency. I can find myself scouring the Downtown Eastside on short notice for a crib, or buying books of transit tickets, or handing out grocery vouchers to people who for any number of reasons have nowhere else to turn. The goal here is to provide assistance with a minimum of red tape and in a way that preserves the client's dignity and self-respect.

In addition to the pastoral role as chaplain, another major area of my responsibility is as coordinator of volunteer services for all of the society's programs. Traditionally, the hospice program has relied heavily on volunteers, but increasingly, more of the society's programs are finding that volunteers can help improve the quality of life for residents and clients. Coordination of volunteer programs is the secular equivalent of "equipping the saints for ministry." It is, in fact, one of the primary roles of any parish priest. Although volunteer programs clearly benefit the society and its clients, they are also of benefit to the volunteers themselves and to the wider community. Volunteer programs at an agency such as St. James Community Service Society tap into people's desire to serve those who are disadvantaged, but they do so in a way that encourages people to build the long-term relationships that are so crucial to making a real difference. Volunteers are asked to make a one-year commitment to the program. As misconceptions are challenged and barriers are broken down, volunteers see the Downtown Eastside as a neighbourhood rather than as a problem. They discover that they are receiving as much as they are giving, and unlikely relationships are built on shared dignity and mutual respect.

There is very little about the work of St. James' Community Service Society or St. James' parish that could be described as dramatically innovative or experimental. "It's the way we've always done it" — or at least the way the Christian church has always aspired to doing it: engaging in prayer, devotion, and works of mercy wherever we find ourselves. It is that rootedness in tradition that gives St. James' its radical and apparently innovative edge. Its refusal to engage in service without the devotional life of office, mass, and rosary to undergird and sustain it seems bizarre and quixotic to many in the community service sector, while its simultaneous refusal to pray without articulating and responding to the manifold needs of the community in which it lives still manages to irritate those who want a more "spiritual" expression of the gospel.

It would be a mistake, though, to think that the ministry of St. James Community Service Society and of St. James' parish in the Downtown Eastside is primarily about "ministering to" the community with the goal of solving its problems. Ministry, like worship, is about encountering the living Christ and being transformed by him. Christ dwells most especially with those who are despised, rejected, or feared by "the rest of us." In our encounters with the addicted, the mentally ill, and the dying, we encounter Christ. To the extent that we allow "them" to minister to "us," we will find ourselves challenged, judged, and forgiven at the deepest levels of our being.

New Westminster Reachout

Kimiko Karpoff

When I asked Dan (not his real name) how he used to spend his days, he couldn't remember. This and that. Whatever. He remembers feeling a lot of anger. Since giving up his welding business because of illness, he has felt frustrated and at loose ends. Now he and his partner, Brenda, live on a disability income.

Several years ago word of mouth led them to the community lunch at St. Barnabas Church, one of three free meals in New Westminster initiated by New Westminster Reachout. They came for the food. They enjoyed the opportunity to visit with folks and get news of the community, and occasionally they sought help through the Reachout office, but mostly it was the food that brought them.

When Reachout staff organized an open meeting after one of the lunches to discuss poverty issues and gauge the community's interest in starting an anti-poverty group, Dan and Brenda decided to check it out.

New Westminster Reachout grew from the vision of a small inner city parish under the leadership of the Rev. Elizabeth Beale. St. Barnabas Church has been called the heart of the Brow of the Hill, a neighbourhood in New Westminster known for ageing woodframe apartments, transiency, unemployment, single parenthood, and single person households. Studies by our regional health authority show that New Westminster has high rates of teen pregnancy, drug overdose, mental illness, and suicide.

But like most cities, New Westminster is full of contrast and contradiction. Juxtaposed to the Brow are the beautiful large heritage homes of the Queen's Park neighbourhood. It's both an old city with a proud history as British Columbia's first capital and a small town where many families have bragging rights that reach back several generations. Located at the geographic centre of BC's lower mainland, it is also the hub of a much larger cosmopolitan area. It is a community struggling to hold onto its traditional understanding of itself while reality changes within and around it.

The folks at St. Barnabas saw a need to engage the community in the task of recognizing its own identity and needs. Through Reachout, they opened their doors to those who needed a place to belong, while opening a dialogue with the community at large.

The Reachout model partnered charity work, such as community meals and referral information, with community development and proactive social justice advocacy. The outreach workers helped to establish free weekly meals in three churches, including St. Barnabas; looked at alternative food supports such as food buying clubs and community kitchens; and started the Affordable Housing Forum with others in the community.

We saw this as a logical progression. The charity work not only provided needed services but also drew people in. Someone who was not yet ready to ask us for help might come for a hot meal. During the meal, the outreach office was open for information and referrals, and the outreach worker's presence at the meals presented an opportunity to talk informally and to establish a basis for trust.

Community development programs were organized around the meals — programs such as an anti-poverty action and support group, a food buying club, workshops on BC Benefits (welfare) rights and responsibilities, and legal aid. Other community resource providers were invited to participate, such as a community health nurse who came twice a month to distribute information and consult with people who, for various reasons, were not accessing health care.

New Westminster Reachout's workers were successful in convincing city officials of the value of branching out from their usual method of gathering public input — public meetings that disenfranchised people would not attend — by holding discussion sessions during community meals. The transit authority also recognized the value of using a St. Barnabas meal as the venue for one of their information and discussion sessions about the expansion of Skytrain.

Reachout also partnered with St. Barnabas in creating community events to bring people together. Multicultural Nights, Fun Day, and other social activities allowed all folks in the community to meet and share in an informal setting.

Dan became very active in the New Westminster Outreach Action Group, an anti-poverty group that began holding weekly meetings after the community lunch. Involvement in the group, Dan said, "gave me direction and the ability to do what I wanted to do — to take positive action."

After joining the group, Dan participated on a committee with city staff and representatives of social organizations and the business community, spoke at city council meetings on issues such as public nuisance bylaws, and became a board member of the provincial anti-poverty organization, End Legislative Poverty. Along with skills in communications, such as planning, organizing, and running a meeting, he "learned the importance of feeling empowered."

"Reachout and the anti-poverty group have given me a sense of direction. It's been really positive," Dan said. "We feel close to a lot of people at St. Barnabas. There's a great sense of camaraderie. This is the way life should be, to help your fellow person. It's also helped me with my anger by giving me an outlet, like a safety valve for extra energy."

Aside from working on the front line, New Westminster Reachout was a voice speaking from a point of view that is too seldom heard. Outreach workers attended anti-poverty rallies, public hearings on neighbourhood issues, and city council meetings, encouraging others from the community to come and speak up. They gave presentations to city committees on issues such as affordable housing and homelessness. They also produced a regular column, "Reaching Out," in the local newspaper.

The "Reaching Out" columns covered issues ranging from the realities that make it difficult for homeless people to get off the street, and how our systems collude to keep poor people powerless, to how one man found the confidence in himself to become a community leader. It profiled people whose mere survival was heroic, and praised community events that brought people together.

The column looked at current issues from different angles. As communities in the lower mainland voiced their concern about nuisance behaviour on our public transit system, with some suggesting that public transit should be reduced, "Reaching Out" noted that public transit simply transports people, whether of good or ill intent, and does not cause panhandling and drug dealing. These problems do not disappear by simply stopping public transit, but need to be addressed at their roots.

"Reaching Out" struck a balance between stories about injustices and other serious concerns, and positive community good news. For example, some columns praised volunteers and their value to communities, while others criticized the increasing need for volunteers as government policy downloads responsibility onto non-profit organizations and churches.

The strength of New Westminster Reachout was in the creation of a continuum. People came to receive an act of charity, but found something more. They found a community of acceptance, an advocate, and the resources to begin making changes in their own lives. The community at large gained a resource that not only provided services to the poor, but also raised awareness of poverty issues by presenting different points of view and encouraging greater understanding.

The sad news is that New Westminster Reachout has closed its doors. Ultimately, the diversity that made Reachout what it was also led to its cessation. For many people, including some members of Reachout's board of directors, the question of charity versus justice was difficult to bridge. While charity is seen as doing something concrete, justice is much more abstract. Charity is unquestionably good, while working for social justice is seen as potentially controversial. Funders like to know how many individuals are fed. Justice work rarely produces easily quantifiable results. Some felt that community development and justice work should be downplayed and charity increased in order to attract funders. Conflicts created by this fundamental chasm distracted board energy away from important issues, such as doing the fundraising. A funding crisis in December 1999 led to the decision to close the doors.

There was more to the dissolution of Reachout than that, of course. The enthusiasm and commitment of board members was not enough to overcome a lack of clearly defined policies and procedures — an ongoing issue. Insufficient staff was another problem: throughout Reachout's six-year history, there was never more than one full-time equivalent staff person at a time. Also, some individuals were too quick to see crisis as failure rather than a wake up call. The church bureaucracy was slow to respond when crisis hit. And there was a lack of faith. By the latter, I mean that budget decisions and planning came from what in Jubilee terms we call "responding from fear of scarcity" rather than the belief in God's abundance. Money fears cast a shadow that stultified the organization's ability to dream, plan, and move forward.

Yet the closure of Reachout cannot be called a failure, nor should it warn anyone away from the Reachout model and philosophy. It does, however, illustrate the need for clarity of vision and the problem that arises when concern over money supersedes philosophy. Rather than a failure, the story of Reachout is a lesson, both in how it worked and how it did not.

After a yuletide visit home, Dan was obviously itching to tell me something. "This was the best Christmas I can remember," he said, smiling, his voice choked with emotion. "My parents told me that they were proud of me. This is the first time they've ever said that.

"It's because of the work I'm doing with Reachout and the Outreach Action Group," he added. "It was the best Christmas."

Reachout's legacy remains. The three community meals continue, run by their host churches. People in the community now feel justified and able to speak up about what they want for the neighbourhood, and for themselves. There is a more open attitude to hearing alternative voices in our local government and community. Reachout's work and voice have also led many churches to revisit their roles in community — and not just in the Anglican parishes. We've been approached by many churches who have realized that they've become too insular and, perhaps, too afraid to rock a boat that needs rocking.

Of course, as always, the need for the work continues. St. Barnabas Church continues to move ahead with the community and justice legacy that it launched in Reachout. There are many who would like to see the Reachout model re-established in New Westminster and established in other communities. With faith, hard work, and the knowledge of lessons learned, perhaps that will happen.

Mile End Community Mission
Montreal

Roslyn Macgregor

The Spirit of the Lord is upon me, because the Lord has anointed me; he has sent me to bring good news to the oppressed, to bind up the broken-hearted, to proclaim liberty to the captives, and release to the prisoners (Isaiah 61:1 and Luke 4:18–19).

Poverty … from those who know:

> "Often the world sees us as less than nothing because we aren't on the same social level as they are."

> "People think that because we are on welfare, we have no value and we know nothing."

> "Often at the grocery store people stare at us. People make judgements, often without knowing what is behind what they see."

> "Beauty is not just what is seen from the exterior. Most of the time, the interior is more beautiful, but is it seen by some?"

LIVING WITH INSECURITY

A good friend asked recently if I thought it might be time to move on to some other ministry. My immediate response was, "No! I love what I'm doing and I'm good at it. It's a wonderful opportunity: vibrant, challenging, often joyous and laughter-filled."

There are also frustrations, and sometimes anger. Community ministry requires a willingness to live with questions that have no clear answers. It can be isolating and disturbing. What is our support — emotional, spiritual, financial — in ministry with the marginalized? It would be simplistic to say that all we need is spiritual support. After all, we trust God, don't we? The reality is that human support, institutional support, and security of funding also matter. All aspects of support are intertwined. Some insecurity and uncertainty is natural; some is unnecessary.

I also serve as a half-time priest also of a small traditional parish, and in that capacity I am aware that, if I have a conflict or challenge in the parish, there are any number of people to whom I can go to talk it over. But the mission is different from a traditional parish, and help isn't as easy to find. Even though there are other community or neighbourhood ministries in Montreal and elsewhere, none has exactly the same focus and vision. While I (as director), and those who work with me, can be energized by time spent with others involved in urban ministry, we have to learn to trust the truth that arises out of the process of our mission ministry at the mission. The vision develops as we go, so we live in faith within one of many dynamics of insecurity. This I see as part of our call — a willingness to trust that God is in the unfolding.

There is often a profound sense of isolation, which sometimes leads to a faltering of trust. This trust is often renewed when we get together with others living the same questions. I believe that those of us in community ministry, or other alternative ministries, would benefit if we had a support network within the church. I don't know what this would look like, but I am ready to explore.

Does the church (administration and general population) understand ministry outside the "norm" of traditional parish ministry? I believe the church wants new ministries to happen. The diocese of Montreal has been financially committed to Mile End Community Mission, and yet we experience a continual and basic sense of insecurity. What happens to the mission seems to reflect a systemic problem in, and challenge to, the church as a whole — a seeming ambivalence about ministries on the "fringe." This ambivalence is expressed in a tendency to promise, and even give, financial support, while at the same time allowing a sense of insecurity in funding. Tensions and uncertainty in funding, and no long-term commitment, make it difficult to plan and to move ahead with some confidence.

How did we get here? A brief history

In the early 1980s, Elaine Pountney, wife of the then rector of the Church of the Ascension, began a ministry of food in a very small storefront not far from the church. Soup and sandwiches were provided to anyone who came. The founding grant ended after several years, and the number of people served had increased beyond the capacity of the space; so the ministry moved to the Church of the Ascension basement.

John Beach became rector in 1985 and the outreach ministry continued. In 1991, the Church of the Ascension was sold to the City of Montréal to be renovated into a library. (The rectory of the Ascension would be sold in 1996.) Since the diocese of Montreal uses interest from the sales of church properties for ministry in the area, some of the interest has been used to support continued outreach to the people of Mile End. John's vision was to create a storefront church with low maintenance costs, and this came into being in 1991 with a food bank, daily lunches, a coffee house, and a Thursday eucharist.

The dream was wonderful, but when John resigned in 1995 to take up another ministry, and I arrived, it was clear that we had to look carefully at how to build for the future on the foundation already laid.

I began by strengthening the board of directors of the mission, and we started to take more responsibility for our own financial matters. Over the next few years, we had some assistance with conflict management, and also held a visioning workshop to which community members, as well as members of the mission, were invited. It became clear that the director was responsible for too much of the operation, and others offered to assume more responsibility. We created bilingual bylaws for operation, got the mission incorporated, began an annual fundraising effort, and applied for our own charity number. The mission became classified in the canons of the diocese of Montreal as a pastoral community, giving us one lay and one clergy member of synod.

In 1998, the building in which we rented space was bought by new owners. In September 1999, we moved next door to 99 Bernard ouest, into a light clean larger space that opened up all sorts of possibilities. We received a very generous grant from the Anglican Foundation to help equip the new kitchen. We have since received increased funding from the diocese of Montreal. Yet even now the future is uncertain.

How are we "church"? Some of the questions

Go out and preach the Gospel. If necessary, speak (St. Francis of Assisi).

How are we called to be church, to live the good news of Jesus Christ in this community? In the first years, we were cautious in how we defined our ministry as "church." Defining ourselves too narrowly might limit our ability to reach out to many of those in need. But if we define ourselves too loosely, are we being church at all? All other questions of identity seem to be lived at the heart of this central one.

Is the mission Anglican? Yes, but what does that mean in the mission setting? Most of the people to whom we minister are not Anglican, yet they have come to see the mission as a spiritual home and refuge. Others continue to attend their own churches on Sundays, yet come to our services as well. Still others live other faith traditions. We are called to be church in the midst of this community. What is our ministry? What are the concrete, as well as spiritual, needs of this "fringe" community? How are we, as church, called to respond? Are we called to provide necessities of living and possibilities for change? We live an Advent — watchful and waiting as we minister, open to new ways to reach out, or to change the old ways.

What is Christian community? We live within a tension of being Christian yet not calling everyone to embrace the Christian faith. We are Christian, yet at the same time people of all faiths are welcome to be part of us. At our Christmas Dinner for 250+ held at the local YMCA last year, a Muslim couple brought their small son, even though it was Ramadan. What a wonderful witness that these parents sat, fasting, through a delicious turkey dinner so that their son could share the feast and receive a gift from Santa Claus.

Where is Jesus? We believe Jesus is with the marginalized — those who are relatively powerless in society, who need someone to stand with them, to advocate for them, to help them speak for themselves. This is the focus of our ministry. It raises questions: What does God's call for justice require of us in this situation? Realistically, how involved can we be, since we are small and few?

We have held funerals, memorial services, baptisms, and a marriage. There is an informal Thursday eucharist and adult Bible study. Christian education for children, however, remains a challenge. Since the children are at school on Thursdays, they attend only special services, such as Christmas Eve, the Easter Vigil, and baptisms, and a few attend Sunday services at other churches. We've had some weekends and days away for confirmation preparation, as well as inviting small confirmation groups from other parishes to the mission. For two years we had Tuesday School after regular school hours. I wonder if we might, in time, create a program at the school for those who wish it.

When asked, How are we "church," some of our members responded:

> We share a vision with the rest of the church even though we worship in a storefront that used to be a crack house. Our worship is simple.

> Everyone shares about the meaning of the gospel. We share food, including spiritual food.

> We're all trying to love one another as God loves us.

How do we give?

The hand that gives is always higher than the hand that receives (African proverb).

We are all children of God and equal in God's sight. But how do we live so that it's a reality and not a patronizing platitude? We're equal, and we're not equal. I have a car. I have a salary that enables me to make choices that many can't.

What does it mean to be poor? What does it mean to give and to receive? We start by listening. Victoria John (aged 13 at the time) wrote the following article for our newsletter:

> Poverty is a word I hate because I live it. I hate it because my mom and my brothers and me suffer each day because of it. I don't have choices.... I take only what is given to me. I feel bad inside and want to lie to my friends and let them think I am like them. I know my family is judged and people look down at us.

I am angry because my mom works harder than most people who has a job and she has nothing. I see her not eat at times to make sure her children can. She never drinks milk. It's always for us. I see how hard it is for her to reach out for help when I know that she just wants to take care of her family....

Poverty to me means never having something you want ,only what someone wants to give to you. I am told always to say Thank You to the people who help me and I am thankful but it hurts....

Poverty means suffering and pain and losing something inside of you like when you go outside you think people can tell I am poor....

Poverty means you have no choices.... I know that money can't buy you happiness, but it can buy you pride.

What are our own power dynamics in giving and receiving? We *like* to give. We all have a *need* to give. Giving, however, places us in a position of power. How do we create a community in which all give and all receive?

In 1995, every week on the day that the food bank was open, we had to find transportation to travel to Moisson Montréal (Montreal Harvest) to pick up the food to be distributed. I often drove my car there until I eventually decided this wasn't a good use of my time. In January 1996, we hired Gardemanger pour tous to pick up and deliver our food, as they do for many community organizations. As a result of this decision, we receive better quality, and greater quantities of, food. This decision provided the opportunity to ask another question: Should we continue to simply give the food away? We chose instead to ask each individual or family to pay fifty cents a week. This money, when totalled at the end of the year, was almost exactly the amount needed to cover the Gardemanger's cost for transportation!

The following year, people did not always keep their commitment. At the annual meeting, the financial statement showed that the food bank had a deficit of $500, exactly the amount needed to pay Gardemanger. An outsider said, "They're poor. They can't afford to pay. The food should be free." Then the people of the mission gave their response — there was an immediate upswing in the weekly contributions, and no deficit ensued. Paying for the transportation of their own food was a symbol of self-respect and of the respect in which we hold them. The uncertainty in making this kind of decision surfaces regularly, and it should. It means we're still listening.

We've wrestled with various ways of operating the food bank. Connie Olson, its director, came up with a solution that has made an enormous difference in attitude. Originally, numbers were given out so that the workers (all of whom are members of the mission and benefit from it as well as "doing" ministry) would know how many bags to prepare. Since we moved into our new quarters, the space is large enough that people can sit and wait, drink coffee, chat, play cards ... people don't have to leave immediately. They can come earlier, and now they give their *names*. No more pushing, struggling to be first. Most important, the solution came from within, and was an opportunity to affirm leadership abilities.

WHO'S IN CHARGE?
I AM, BUT.... WE ALL ARE, BUT....

Well, really, God's in charge, but that can too easily be a religious-sounding cop-out and an avoidance of taking responsibility. I'm in charge, but how do I accept my own responsibility while at the same time encouraging the leadership of others?

In a parish, one can normally identify some who can be asked to take certain responsibilities, and expect that they will carry them out. At the mission, there is first a long process of encouragement and support. Sometimes, when I have recognized an ability in someone, I have encouraged them to "go for it." After a time, I've discovered that those involved need to learn some basic skills (for example, in communication of concrete needs or wishes) before they are ready to "take off on their own." For instance, a committee was formed to coordinate community suppers. Some people who are strong, competent, and good cooks (!) may not realize that it's better to tell others that they are needed at 4:00 to set up, and still others at 7:00 for clean-up, rather than being annoyed at not having enough help.

Being human, we sometimes even create situations in which we are overwhelmed. My role is, in part, to provide alternative ways of interacting and working together. I need often to clarify situations and to name behaviours that aren't helpful. Except in certain situations, change can't be required, and as we grow together, I try to model change and to be patient with myself and with others. At present, relationships, community building, and improved communications are more important than creating new programs. This has meant a slow approach to beginning most new ventures. Should there be more programs going? Programs could certainly be a visible sign that the ministry is working. We're committed to community building and believe that, if we build a strong foundation with more leaders, programs will grow.

Who's in charge? For someone who often likes (sometimes feels she needs, which isn't the same thing) to be in control, leadership issues are a constant challenge. This is particularly true in a community of people whose lives are mainly crisis-oriented. I find that sometimes I have tried to share leadership, but ended up being "dishonest" and unclear about expectations. This wasn't fair to anyone. Sharing and building leadership can happen if I'm willing to accept my own responsibility for being truthful and clear.

Do we have to be crisis-oriented?

When we live from day to day, from crisis to crisis, we don't know other ways of relating to or in the world. If there isn't a crisis, we can always create one! There's a certain stability in living the way we're used to. One goal of the mission is to provide alternatives to crisis-oriented living. In the beginning, someone would say, for instance: "The kettle has disappeared! Someone must have taken it!" I would bite the hook and say, "Oh, no! Who could have done that?! Why?!" Age, experience, increasing wisdom (and a strong desire to preserve my sanity) have led me to a different approach: "Oh. That's too bad, what shall we do?" The kettle would often turn up later in the basement or elsewhere. Even if it didn't, getting caught up in the crisis wasn't helpful to any of us. I've also chosen gently and directly to confront the person creating the crisis. My refusal to get excited has a calming influence, not least on myself, and it makes a calm reasonable approach seem normal.

What's "normal"? Should everyone's life and situation be like ours?

Middle-class helpers also struggle with the question of whether to impose our view of normal on others. For example, Mary, one of our mission members, has been hospitalized with serious illness. She requires some monitoring, but is able to maintain her independence. Her thinking is disorganized, and she finds it difficult, but not impossible, to maintain her home. How do we assist without intruding? How do we help her maintain her independence and basic levels of health and cleanliness without expecting that everyone should have the same standards of housekeeping and personal hygiene that we might think essential? How do we live in the paradox that this person has the right to make her own personal decisions, without imposing our own values?

I recently discussed the situation with Mary's social worker and we then visited Mary in her apartment. With Mary's help, we did what we could to restore some basic health and safety standards, and accompanied her to the clinic to have her physical ailment treated. She might be "better off" in some form of sheltered living. On the other hand, she lives in a community that she knows and finds stabilizing, and she shouldn't be forced out of it. She regards the mission as a home and her family. Mary's right to independence outweighs our desire for her to live a more "normal" life. And at the crux of the matter is this question: What is normal? Upper-middle class standards of living?

ARE WE IN IT ALONE?

We are working in various ways to break our sense of isolation. We have developed, and continue to develop, links with the local CLSC (community health resource), YMCA, Eco-Quartier, Cuisines collectives de Québec, and other organizations. We're working with the police to develop the protocol for screening volunteers. For two years I have been a community representative on the governing board of the neighbourhood English school, and recently became a member of the newly formed Comité des partenaires aviseurs, for our local police station. These positions allow me both to present the concerns of people in the community and to work together with others to address the concerns. We also have creative relationships with a number of parishes in the diocese, and these need to be nurtured and developed because the mission is a ministry of the diocese in the inner city, and the challenge is to educate others to recognize the ministry as theirs also.

Questions of Language and Belonging

All of the political realities of Quebec and — effectively — of our changing world, are lived at the mission in microcosm. Language is a challenge and constant source of tension (not necessarily a bad thing) on many different levels. We work bilingually, usually happily, and by choice. We accommodate, as we are able, those speaking other languages, since we minister in a multi-ethnic community. Biweekly staff meetings are intentionally bilingual. I speak in both languages, and one of the members often acts as translator during these meetings when necessary. This encourages the use of others' gifts — not a small thing for someone with little formal education but with an ability to translate.

We have, in effect, two "matriarchs" at the mission, both of whom are volunteers. Church people know the difficulties of there being more than one matriarch in a community. One is unilingually French speaking, the other, English speaking with some French. Each is responsible for her own aspects of the ministry, but tensions do arise between individuals and between the two groups. Envy and perceptions of favoured treatment are registered by both groups, coloured by prior and present experiences of discrimination in Quebec. I try to keep the issues in the open. Staff meetings are used to encourage us to speak our minds directly to each other, rather than allowing resentments to fester and destroy relationships. Issues related to language won't go away — and in my better moments, I welcome them. We're alive and well! And if there weren't conflict over language, there would be about something else. I suspect that, in addition to language, the tensions are, at a very basic level, simply ways of living out a competition for love, respect, and acceptance.

CHALLENGES FOR THE FUTURE

We have entered a new century with the aim of creating a stable funding base so that much of the energy currently used for survival can be redirected into pastoral, educational, and other aspects of the ministry

A few days ago, the staff went to the Sisters of St. John the Divine in St. Lambert for a picnic. We all started out rather grumpy and wrapped up in our own little worlds. Three of us have teenagers, and it was report card day. We shared stories of children and teens, then ate a lovely lunch together, laughed and played. A watermelon seed spitting contest is a great leveller! I realized we need to get away and to have fun together more often.

GOD HAS MOVED INTO THE NEIGHBOURHOOD

Ministry of Presence in Weston, Toronto

Mark Kinghan

I heard a voice thunder from the Throne: Look! Look! God has moved into the neighbourhood, making his home with men and women! (Revelation 21 from Eugene Peterson's *The Message*).

Revelation 21, as translated by Eugene Peterson, reflects a theology of ministry that calls the church to be God's presence in the communities where we are situated. Our church buildings, and our worshipping congregations, are one form of an important and vital presence we can have in our neighbourhoods. If church congregations remain isolated and inward looking, however, solely focusing on themselves and their own needs, then they miss a tremendous opportunity to serve and witness to their faith in ways that make real differences in the lives of those who live, walk, and work outside the church. For many reasons, people may find it difficult to enter a church. As a result, we as the church need to find ways to be where people are, on their ground, in their community.

The town of Weston is part of the City of Metropolitan Toronto. It is also a neighbourhood with a real spirit of community and identity. This has been a benefit in enabling the church to be present, visible, and active in the life of the community, and to be recognized as a vital part of the fabric of the neighbourhood. The Weston Road corridor is lined with high-rise apartments, small businesses, and a deteriorating downtown. Demographically, there is a high rate of poverty and incidence of single parent families, and an increasing number of new immigrants and seniors on low fixed incomes. Drugs, prostitution, crime, and violence have led to feelings of insecurity and fear.

Off the main street is another neighbourhood: established Weston, with old single-family homes, schools, and parks. Many who reside here are long time residents: both seniors who are able to maintain their homes, and young professionals who grew up in Weston and have decided to raise their families here. These neighbourhoods, with such a diverse mixture of people, are St. John's mission field.

In 1996, St. John's vestry endorsed an intentional ministry of presence in the community of Weston. Every Thursday morning, the incumbent could be found walking the streets, sitting in Burger King, or having coffee in the Central Restaurant. This came to be known as our "hanging out" ministry, and that's exactly what it was. Although it was the incumbent who was out in the community, this ministry was regarded as the ministry of the whole parish. By "hanging out" in places where the community gathered together, it afforded us the opportunity to interact with people who would likely never darken the doors of our church building.

On Thursday mornings, Burger King is a gathering spot for lonely seniors who go there to be lonely together; on the streets are the poor asking for money to buy a cup of coffee; in the local donut store are the unemployed and those on disability who have nowhere else to go. In each of these places, community is formed as people in similar life situations find one another and build relationships. It was a privilege to be allowed into the lives of these people, and given a place where, on the surface, we didn't seem to fit. As a rapport of trust and respect was established, opportunities arose to listen to people's stories. We began to learn who was in our community, and something about the lives they lived and the challenges they faced.

At the same time as we were meeting the disenfranchised of society, contacts were also being made with people of influence, the decision makers in the community. The Central Restaurant is where local politicians, representatives of the neighbourhood rate-payers association, the Lions Club, the Business Improvement Association, and the police gather. As a result of our becoming acquainted with these people, the invitation was extended to our parish to be involved in community events as the area church representative. We were asked to sit on community committees that dealt with issues such as safety and crime, cleaning up the appearance of Weston, and the local impact of government decisions concerning health care, education, and social services. In so doing, we were able to raise awareness of community and political issues in the parish, to pray about them as part of our Sunday morning worship, and to encourage individuals in our church to take them seriously. All of this helped us to realize that the more connected we were with the community, the more we were empowered to speak out against the wrongs and injustices we saw and heard about.

As our "hanging out" ministry was taking shape, the parish made a commitment to a ministry of hospitality and outreach. "Com Sup" is a community supper held each Thursday evening, at which anyone is welcome to eat at no charge. This ministry is lay led and lay run, with a volunteer base of approximately forty individuals. The volunteers are parishioners of St. John's, members of another local congregation, interested people from the community, and our guests who have decided they would like to do something to help. After being in operation for five years, we now serve on average sixty to eighty people each week, including up to ten children. Our guests come for various reasons: those on social assistance who are unable to make ends meet; the working poor whose rent each month takes the majority of their wages; the lonely who need someone to sit and talk and share a meal with; the homeless who are looking for somewhere warm for a few hours on a cold evening. Everyone who comes has some need. We may never know what that need is, but the important thing is that people come to our church hall to share this time.

Over the last five years, a real sense of community has developed at Com Sup. Initially, people would come, eat, and leave for home. Now they arrive early, arrange tables together for their friends, and stay late talking, sharing, and caring for one another. In addition to a nourishing meal, donations of clothes are available to those who need them, and leftover food is sent home with anyone who wants it.

We might be tempted to think of ourselves as superior to those we serve; that we the church are doing something wonderful for them; that they can see the face of Christ in us as we reach out and serve them. In truth, we receive blessings ourselves from this ministry. The greatest gift is that, in serving out the meat and potatoes or pasta and sauce, we are feeding Christ himself. Until we became involved in Com Sup, meeting the individuals who came, and hearing the struggles of their lives, it was easy to be judgemental of the people standing in front of the store asking for spare change. It wasn't hard to turn and walk away, and even think badly about why they were in that position in the first place. But once we sat down and shared a meal with them, once we called them by name, we had no choice but to see them as human beings — people in real need. What a privilege it is to serve in this kind of ministry and listen to the stories of our guests! Every Thursday in our parish hall, we are standing on holy ground, encountering the living and suffering Christ right here in our midst.

Just as Com Sup has taught us that ministries of outreach can become ministries of fellowship, we have also learned that ministries of fellowship can become ministries of outreach. We have seen this happen with two groups that meet regularly at St. John's: a monthly lunch for seniors known as the OWLS (Older, Wiser, Livelier Seniors) and our weekly Friday Night Euchre. Both of these activities were initially set up to meet the fellowship needs of parishioners. Over time, however, we have seen an increase in community participation in both these groups. Where other organizations and institutions have retired these kinds of programs because of lack of funds and volunteers, we have been able to fill the gap. These two ministries are an overwhelming success as ministries of presence and outreach, meeting an obviously increasing need for fellowship within the community.

As we began these ministries of presence at St. John's, it was important to reflect on our motivation. First, we recognized that reaching out and being present cannot simply come out of our need to survive as a church. If we do these ministries because our numbers are down, or because our Sunday collection isn't high enough, then we are doing them for the wrong reasons. Our experience has re-enforced the fact that community ministries of presence are about the mission of the gospel and not the maintenance of the institution. Our goal could not be simply to bring people into the church, although that has been a spin-off we have enjoyed. The primary goal of any ministry of presence needs to be to meet people where they are, to deal with their issues, not our own.

Second, we have learned that our primary task is not to convert those we meet by the traditional means of evangelism. Our faith is evident in what we are doing and why we are doing it; often, actions give a clearer message than any words we might speak. If opportunities arise, we do talk about issues of faith and spirituality. On more than one occasion we have been asked to conduct memorial services and funerals for individuals who have had no church connection. We have been invited into these sacred moments in people's lives because they knew that we would meet them where they were and allow them to express their grief in ways that were appropriate to their given situation. In sharing these holy moments, we have had avenues for telling the gospel story of God's love for all people, even and especially for those whom the rest of society ridicules, shuns, and ignores. In these moments of pain and suffering, perhaps the good news of the gospel has intersected their own life stories, and they have heard a word of hope and peace. Rather than preaching to them, our ministry of presence involves walking with them.

A further spin-off of St. John's ministry of presence was the invitation from the community to participate in The Weston End of Summer Blast. This began with a representative of St. John's being included in the planning process for this community festival. Out of the initial planning came the request for a gospel service in the park, to which the whole community would be invited. Representatives of the area churches, through the leadership of St. John's, accepted the invitation to be an ecumenical presence at this event in the life of our neighbourhood. The first year, we hosted a gospel concert and service, using the talent of local congregations; the second year, the Gospel Festival was conducted on a larger scale, including a professional gospel singer. It was wonderful to be present, visible, and recognized as a Christian presence in this secular event.

Out of our involvement in the Blast, the area churches recognized our potential ministry of presence and evangelism through a united witness to our faith. The result was the formation of The Christian Community Connection, with representation from each of the seven mainline churches in the Weston area. After working closely together for two years, our mandate is to reach out in faith to our community as a visible and recognized Christian presence. Our goals are to foster supportive relationships among the churches of Weston, and to build strong church–community connections. We continue to accomplish this by planning summer services in an area park, Good Friday walks, Easter sunrise services, Christmas caroling in the streets, and a presentation of "Bethlehem Live" in partnership with a local theatre group. As individual churches, our presence might be minimal and perhaps unnoticed.

By working together, we can have a much greater impact. We are more visible as the body of Christ, making God's presence more recognized in our neighbourhood.

These kinds of ministries do not happen overnight, without any kind of struggle. It takes patience and a willingness to stay in the trenches, as uncomfortable as it may feel. Building the relationships necessary to be present, active, visible, and recognized in the wider community takes time; it's an investment we have to keep making in the life of the church. Even though as a parish we are ensconced in our ministries of presence in the community, we still struggle to discern where God is calling us to go next and how we might build on what we have so that we can be more effective in reaching those we meet and in helping them more with their issues and concerns. A big part of the difficulty in moving forward, though, is how much one church can do on its own; and furthermore, how often we can continue to tap the same volunteers whose energy is already overextended. In addition, the question remains, how to balance parish needs with community needs. As well, delving more into the realm of community ministry takes us farther outside the box of what parish ministry traditionally has been. These kinds of changes in direction can cause conflict. Change can be difficult, especially when there is concern that something might be given up.

There are no right answers to any of these questions and concerns. There is also no one formula to use when beginning community ministries of presence in the first place. One thing we have learned out of our experience is that eventually you have to stop reflecting and talking about community ministry, and start doing it. We in the church need to be willing to take the risk of doing things differently with faith and trust. Community ministry is about being guided by God's Spirit to discern how we can do our part in building up the kingdom of God in our neighbourhoods. The church, in every community and neighbourhood, needs to be willing to take the risks and leaps of faith necessary to venture into the unknowns so that God can have an address in every neighbourhood. We need to trust that God, working through us, can and will do more than we can ask or imagine. As others begin to recognize the face of Christ in us, we need to look for the face of Christ in them.

The world may say that the church isn't relevant any longer, but if we take hold of the Spirit and follow where we're led, then the church will be resurrected, and we will experience the new life that only God can give. The church will be renewed and revitalized as we remain open to the neighbourhood ministries of presence God is calling us to. As we venture outside the walls of our buildings, we need to listen in our neighbourhoods, and to rejoice and celebrate as we hear the voices around us saying: "Look! Look! God has moved into our neighbourhood, making his home with us!"

INDIGENOUS MINISTRY

The case studies of Indigenous ministry that follow are about models of education and formation rather than models of pastoral care, liturgy, or "ministry delivery." This is consistent with the notion that, when people select and appoint leaders from their own numbers, and take responsibility for their learning, they become deeply engaged in the process of forming community and affirming identity. Putting resources and care into ministry formation is also in keeping with the movement among Indigenous communities in Canada to strive for self-determination and equal partnership according to their own cultural values.

The following reflections, which form an introduction to this section, are taken from a paper by the Rev. Canon Fletcher Stewart, prepared for the Churches' Council on Theological Education in Canada, 1 December 1996.

In the late 1800s, the Church Mission Society (CMS) undertook mission based on the principle that every nation should develop a national church reflective of its distinctive ethos. Such churches would become "self-governing, self-supporting, and self-propagating." The colonial era introduced an extended detour, but there is evidence of attempts to reclaim that goal.

One of the legacies of the colonial experience is a tension between faith and culture. Nowadays we often refer to a process of enculturation, in which Christian faith is progressively incarnated in a particular culture: first by linguistic translation, then by partial adaptation to local custom, then through indigenization or replacing outside missionaries with Indigenous personnel, and finally through complete enculturation in which faith and culture reach a new synthesis.

In the colonial era, however, the gospel was introduced into First Nations as a force over and against Indigenous culture. Although the process of translation was effectively launched, and a lot of unconscious adaptation took place, there was little intentional thought of adapting or indigenizing the gospel to fit into traditional culture. In most cases, there was no attempt to "discern the spirits" within Indigenous beliefs. Rather, the tendency was to make a wholesale condemnation of all Indigenous spirituality as pagan and demonic.

Many First People are now striving to recover their lost heritage. Words like "traditional" and "culture" are commonly used among First Nations in reference to their Indigenous usages, customs, and religion. Yet in many communities, the local Elders are Christian traditionalists, whose heritage is the Cree Prayer Book and Hymn Book, and who are very suspicious of the demonic potential of the "old ways."

This creates a crisis within Indigenous communities. Indigenous Christians now have a second opportunity to exercise discernment around these questions. But they are deeply divided as to how to integrate Indigenous customs and beliefs with Christian faith and practice. It is hard for people of European culture to appreciate the agony for traditionally tight-knit communities who find themselves divided along spiritual lines in this way. Donna Bomberry, Indigenous ministries coordinator of the Anglican Church of Canada, calls this struggle "spiritual warfare," and considers it to be part of the deep work of healing and reconciliation.

This also presents an issue for training programs such as the ones described here. In certain places, such as the Dr. Jessie Saulteaux Resource Centre, there has been considerable effort to introduce and understand such traditions as the Medicine Wheel. The Native Ministries Consortium at Vancouver School of Theology, for example, introduces students to the spiritual traditions of the coastal people.

The attitude of mainstream society is mixed. Indigenous ceremonies can still create uneasiness among church officials and funders. On the other hand, non-Indigenous individuals who wish to be progressive can become enthusiastic supporters of cultural practices of which they have little understanding. It is all too easy for those who are members of the dominant culture to assume that they are the ones responsible for solving this problem, rather than to see it as an issue for Indigenous people to tackle among themselves. Training institutions are in a position to facilitate this process, however. An attitude of respect for both cultures, both approaches and traditions, can open up opportunities for individuals to experience and experiment without condemning either tradition.

DR. JESSIE SAULTEAUX RESOURCE CENTRE

Maylanne Maybee with Aileen Urquhart

THE STUDENT BODY

Norway House is an Indigenous community located at the north end of Lake Winnipeg. The local United church is served by the Rev. John Crate, a full-time minister who trained at Cook College and Theological School in Arizona. He is assisted by three students. Olive, a nurse at the health clinic, directs a Sunday school and youth program, gives leadership at home church meetings, and offers important pastoral care in the context of her work. She has also been appointed to lead worship at a small family church tucked away in beautiful bush on Tower's Island, reachable only by boat. Ernest works in the province's Natural Resources department, and gives musical leadership in numerous home services and on the radio. Mary Ann helps with services, care and education of young children, and healing work among the sick.

Round Lake, Saskatchewan, is an Indigenous community that draws from four reserves. Following the prolonged tenure of a non-Indigenous minister, the local United church had come to rely on supply clergy for their pastoral leadership until they approached Hector, a local person attached to the Pentecostal church, and asked if he would be their minister. Hector had been brought up "under care" and had returned to his home community of Round Lake after attending Bible school and becoming a Pentecostal minister. The local United Church presbytery required him to attend the Dr. Jessie Saulteaux Resource Centre. Although the theology and values of the centre initially challenged Hector's Pentecostal background, he has appreciated the opportunity to learn more, and in turn, his home community has developed and grown.

Maria is the full-time student minister of Regina Native Outreach Ministry, which offers pastoral care and a worship sharing circle for Indigenous people who live in Regina and the surrounding reserves. Darlene volunteers with this ministry, and has run a children's program. Though one is in a paid ministerial placement and the other is a volunteer, both are accountable for their work, are expected to set learning goals, and are supported in their work and study by their "vision keeper," a person experienced in ministry, often an Elder, who acts as a mentor and fulfills some of the functions of a supervisor.

Learning circles

I met these and several other students when I attended a learning circle at the Dr. Jessie Saulteaux (pronounced *so-toe*) Resource Centre in July 1999. The learning circle was part of the community based Indigenous ministry training program, in which students are required to work at least half-time in ministry (in a congregation, chaplaincy, or a social ministry) over a five-year period. Most are employed as pastors or workers in social service and outreach positions, and then use a combination of study leave, continuing education leave, and holiday time to free themselves for the residential component of the program. Four times a year the students leave their communities to gather at the centre for two weeks of learning circles, during which they study a wide range of topics, including scripture, theology, and ministry formation.

During my week in July 1999, the theme of the learning circle was Indigenous culture and spirituality. In the mornings, we collected willow branches and learned the art of basket making. In the afternoons, two Indigenous Elders and a non-Indigenous Mennonite woman who had become a student of Indigenous spiritual practices came as a visiting resource team. They brought star blanket, pipe, bundle, tobacco, rattle, sweet grass, eagle feather — and gave teachings about the significance and traditional use of these objects in Indigenous spiritual practices. Seated in a circle, the students spoke about what they had seen and heard, one by one, without comment or interruption from the others. Some spoke quietly and briefly; others described and interpreted their dreams, often at considerable length; still others spoke in the eloquent style of the prophets of old. The presentation created some controversy among the students. Many came from communities that had always upheld traditional values and teachings. Others had been brought up in places where traditional teachings were regarded as "the work of the devil." At the Dr. Jessie Saulteaux Resource Centre, both Christian and traditional teachings are honoured, and the centre accepts and lives with the tension this creates. Though the views of the students and their styles of expression differed widely, the tension among them decreased visibly, and their positions became less polarized as they shared around the circle.

It was quite unlike any theological seminar I had ever attended. Besides being fascinated with the subject matter, I was greatly impressed by the respect with which each speaker was received, and by the complexity and nuancing of different viewpoints.

The Dr. Jessie Saulteaux Resource Centre is located near Beausejour, Manitoba, about an hour's drive north of Winnipeg, nestled as a cluster of buildings and lodges next to the Brokenhead River. Visible from the road is a teepee standing in a clearing next to the main lodge, and a walk on the grounds will take you to a sweat lodge. When I visited the centre, I was privileged to be led through a sweat ritual by the Rev. Dr. Stanley McKay, co-director of the centre. The presence of a teepee and sweat lodge indicates the centre's commitment to honour our relationship with the Creator and the wholeness of creation, and the desire to share that perspective with the wider community.

Named after Jessie Saulteaux, a beloved and visionary educator, the centre was founded in the mid-1980s as a place for preparing and supporting Indigenous students for ministry and the communities they serve. Until then, most Indigenous students seeking ordination in the United Church of Canada attended Cook College and Theological School in Arizona. The Resource Centre offered an alternative that would enable Indigenous candidates for ministry to study and prepare for this role without being removed from the communities to which they would relate.

A national consultation of the United Church held in the 1970s helped to establish what would meet the requirements for preparation for the Order of Ministry. Following a period of experimentation, the United Church of Canada now recognizes the centre as being able to satisfy the requirements for ordination and commissioning. Currently seventeen students are enrolled in the centre's program, which is primarily directed to members of the United Church, although Anglican, Lutheran, Mennonnite, and Presbyterian students have also participated.

LIFE AT THE DR. JESSIE SAULTEAUX RESOURCE CENTRE

A typical two-week learning circle at the centre will begin with travel on a Monday, often over long distances, followed the next day by a period of "checking in" at the main community building — an opportunity to rebuild friendships and regain a sense of being part of a learning community. Any given gathering will include about fifteen students, many of whom might come with their children, partner, or extended family members.

An Elder or resource staff member will often be invited to give an introduction to the assigned topic. Students are expected to have completed some advance textbook reading at a level suited to their ability. If necessary, the leader may have gone through the text ahead of time, taking notes or clarifying the language, and producing a twenty- to thirty-page interpretation. Students then work on texts with guided questions in small groups, organized according to language and culture. Small groups will report back and share their learnings with the whole group in some creative way, including drama, music, and art.

The learning circles will often include one week that focuses on some area of theory or scholarship, such as biblical studies or theology, while practical issues such as counselling or administration are the focus during the other week. Pastoral concerns that particularly affect Indigenous communities are given priority, including abuse of alcohol or other intoxicants, or healing from and preventing sexual misconduct, harassment, or abuse.

Class leaders are often, though not always, Indigenous. They may be members of the staff, community Elders, or invited resource people. They will offer teaching and small group leadership in return for an honorarium. Leaders have included such people as Stan McKay, former moderator of the United Church, Gladys Cook, a respected healer who herself experienced childhood sexual abuse and cultural deprivation in a residential school, staff from the Manitoba Addictions Research Foundation, and a faculty member from the history department of the University of Winnipeg.

The centre strives for a balance between theological and pastoral content, and cultural and traditional context. For example, when I visited, a session led by Raymond Beaumont dealt with the history of the Rev. James Evans, a Methodist minister in Norway House in the 1840s. Four young Indigenous women had laid charges of sexual assault against James Evans. The Methodist church investigated the charges, exonerated Evans, and dismissed the young women as troublemakers. Raymond used the opportunity to raise the issue of the importance of sexual and pastoral ethics. In another session, Dr. Jennifer Brown reviewed early baptismal registers from Norway House to show how Cree names that had been written in syllabics had been changed to English names in later registers. Thus someone named "Manatawans" had been re-named "Mason." It was a lesson in history and social analysis with a personal twist.

COURSE DESIGN

The program includes courses in Hebrew and Christian scriptures, doctrine, Christian history, ethics, Christian nurture, and practice of ministry, which are standard in other theological schools. The Dr. Jessie Saulteaux Resource Centre and its sister college in southern Ontario, the Francis Sandy Theological Centre, also include Indigenous traditional teachings, and emphasize First Nations history and culture. Graduates receive a diploma of completion. An additional year of courses qualifies a student for a Bachelor of Theology in partnership with the Faculty of Theology at the University of Winnipeg.

ADMISSION REQUIREMENTS

To be admitted, a student must have at least Grade 12 education, show personal maturity, and give evidence of congregational support. Students are required to link with their presbytery early in the program. The usual pattern is for a person to show interest, to approach a presbytery discernment committee with the support of their congregation, and to move towards a shared understanding of being called. The student will receive funding for their studies through United Church bursaries and band council grants.

Model for Learning

The centre understands and treats students as both learners and teachers. Its approach to learning is based on a methodology of action and reflection — having the students try something in a direct or hands on way, then bringing them together to reflect on common themes and do some form of social analysis. There are no exams — each student is interviewed, and his or her growth is tracked and measured through processes of integration, oversight, progress reports, and evaluation. One course equals one credit. At the Dr. Jessie Saulteaux Resource Centre, each course includes discussions with vision keepers and reflection on learning in field placement, as well as classroom hours. Obtained over five years, the forty-five credits are equivalent to the thirty to thirty-six credits of a conventional residential theological program.

The official processes of the United Church of Canada parallel the learning process at the centre. The conference (roughly equivalent to a diocese) interviews students to determine their suitability and, ultimately, their readiness for ordination. The sponsoring presbytery (a unit smaller than a conference) interviews students annually or less often.

The Centre's Mandate

The Dr. Jessie Saulteaux Resource Centre has a twofold mandate: (1) to prepare First Nations people for ministry, and (2) to facilitate cross-cultural learning for the wider community. The centre is a place of retreat and healing. It offers culturally appropriate learning, leadership development that is based in the local community, spiritual formation that is sensitive to Indigenous ways, and community transformation.

The assumptions behind its program, which to the eyes of a visitor can appear deceptively simple and low key, are that ministry needs to be culturally specific, and it needs to address the social breakdown and economic stagnation that have resulted from years of colonial oppression and racism. Traditional values and spirituality are respected, yet practices such as sweats, smudging, and fasting are always optional, and care is taken to support the cultural and family life of the students. While its primary focus is on the needs of Indigenous students for ministry and the needs of Indigenous communities, it also is a place in the wider church for cross-cultural learning.

At the public graduation ceremony that marks the completion of the program, the students tell the story of the healing journey they have travelled as part of the process of becoming a minister in their community. Their stories highlight the deepest value of the centre: that personal healing and spiritual wholeness, far more than academic achievement or straight As, are what qualify a person for ministry.

KEEWATIN AND TAIP

David N. Ashdown

Today, we stand on the verge of a new millennium. We have two thousand years of Christian witness to support us in our ministry today and as we look to the future. St. Paul tells us, "Therefore, since we are surrounded by so great a cloud of witnesses, let us lay aside every weight and the sin that clings so closely, and let us run with perseverance the race that is set ahead of us looking to Jesus the pioneer and perfecter of our faith" (Hebrews 12:1–2). We too are called to be witnesses to the good news that God was in Christ, reconciling the world to himself, and we have been entrusted with that ministry of reconciliation. The world is as desperate to hear the message we proclaim today as it has been at any time in the past two thousand years. Our tradition is not something from the past to cling to in order to avoid the challenges of the future. Rather, it is the foundation on which we build a new temple for the Lord in our own day. We must not fear change, for the Lord is always calling us to new work (The Rt. Rev. Gordon Beardy, first Indigenous diocesan bishop in the Anglican Church of Canada and a graduate of TAIP (Train an Indigenous Priest); from the Bishop's Charge to the 42nd Session of the Synod of the Diocese of Keewatin, 4 March 2000).

The diocese of Keewatin is extremely diverse. It straddles the two civil provinces: Manitoba and Ontario. It has five languages and cultures: English, Cree, Oji-Cree, Ojibway, and Dené. Its parishes vary from urban communities along major highways to small isolated northern communities, many of which can be reached only by air or by temporary winter roads. Despite all these differences, the people of Keewatin have decided to walk together on their common faith journey in Jesus Christ.

For administrative purposes, the diocese is divided into three regions, each with its own archdeacon. The smallest region, Northern Manitoba, covers the area northeast of Norway House and is predominantly Cree. The largest, Northern Ontario, covers northwestern Ontario, north of Sioux Lookout and Red Lake, and is predominantly Oji-Cree. The Southern Region covers areas in southeastern Manitoba and northwestern Ontario around Kenora-Aitikoken, and is predominantly English.

To minister effectively in such diverse conditions, it is important that clergy be able to speak the language of the communities in which they serve, as well as have some understanding of local culture. Almost from the very beginning of the diocese it was obvious that the conventional pattern of supplying parishes with seminary trained stipendiary clergy would not work. Even when such clergy were available, often they soon became frustrated and overwhelmed, and either left for other appointments or suffered serious burnout.

In 1966, Archbishop Ted Scott, former primate of the Anglican Church of Canada, posed the following question to people across the country:

Is the Church going to move in the direction of seeking to develop responsible, creative leadership in the widest sense of the word or will it continue to focus attention on a narrow concept of institutional ministry?

The diocese of Keewatin responded to this challenge by establishing TAIP (Train An Indian Priest), an ordination program for First Nations persons who had been selected by their community as candidates and would serve without stipends. In 1971, the Indian Advisory Council met with the diocesan bishop, the Rt. Rev. H. Stiff, to advocate a locally raised priesthood that would improve the sacramental and pastoral life of isolated northern congregations. This was a critical issue, since at the time only two clergy were deployed for ministry among twenty-five isolated Indigenous communities. The council, assisted by Michael Peers, then archdeacon of Rupert's Land and a member of the General Synod Committee on Ministry, examined the possibilities that might be available to them through the ministry of financially self-supporting ordained individuals such as trapper priests. Candidates could be chosen by local communities using agreed criteria, and prepared for ordination through a locally designed and delivered training program.

When the diocesan synod endorsed the council's plan in 1972, it began a process that would bring incredible change to the life of the diocese. The first three-year program was a basic course in the Old and New Testament, liturgy, doctrine (with special emphasis on sacraments and the creed), pastoral education, and parish organization. The program began running later that same year at Starr Lake just west of Kenora, and eighteen men selected by their communities attended. Most of these men had already been serving their church as catechists for twenty to forty years. Although few had any formal schooling, most had attended the Dauphin Catechist School, a training program for Indigenous lay readers run as a joint venture by the dioceses of Keewatin, Brandon, and Rupert's Land in the mid-1950s. All were well versed in the scriptures and the *Book of Common Prayer*. Eleven graduates were ordained in 1974, and three more in 1976.

The effects of the first TAIP program were so positive that a ministry consultation in Kitchenuhmaykoosib Inninuwug (Big

Trout Lake) recommended that the program be extended to provide locally raised-up clergy for communities without a priest, and to replace those of the first group who were of retirement age.

As the candidates for the second TAIP were younger and less experienced than their predecessors, the course was lengthened to five years. An assessment committee, including four graduates of TAIP 1, made recommendations on the suitability of graduates of the program for ordination. Fourteen were ordained.

Some flavour of the training is contained in the following description in a diocesan report of the third year summer program:

> In the first week, a great deal of time was spent on the meaning and practice of baptism in the life of the church both past and present, as well as baptism as practised by the new Pentecostals sweeping through the north. Baptismal preparation programs were discussed as well as the students being given the opportunity to examine the type of questions asked of parents and godparents in the new baptismal rite. In the second week, the Rev. Stanley McKay, United Church of Canada Consultant for Native Ministries, conducted a three-day course on Marriage in the Native Community. The changing patterns of marriage relationships … marriage preparation, and support for married couples were some of the topics dealt with by Mr. McKay. Native clergy from our diocese helped to shed light on many of the pastoral concerns faced by the priests and catechists in northern villages. Archdeacon Terry McNear followed this with presentations and discussion on the topic of Remarriage of Divorced Persons in the Church and the process of our church for counselling and the role of the marriage commission.

As is the case with most radical new initiatives, this program came under criticism both from within the diocese and beyond. It was suggested that, because the clergy formed by this process were worker/trapper priests, they would become merely "eucharistizers." Some thought that an order of second class Indigenous priests was being developed simply because they were non-stipendiary. The diocesan leadership, however, made it clear from the beginning that the only difference between a stipendiary priest and a non-stipendiary priest was the amount of time the individual had to commit to priestly work. It also immediately began a process to develop non-stipendiary ordained ministry among its non-Indigenous parishes. Furthermore, while it was initially assumed that clergy trained through TAIP and other non-traditional programs would be non-stipendiary, that assumption has not proved to be true. Today, half of the stipendiary positions in the diocese are filled with non-seminary trained clergy.

Since its inception twenty-eight years ago, TAIP has produced over fifty clergy, most of whom are actively serving in the diocese in all three orders: deacon, priest, and bishop. Its success, however, did not stop there. Once Indigenous people had been ordained, a dramatic increase of interest in lay ministry followed.

A five-year Bible school was initiated in the Northern Ontario region. For two to three weeks each summer, seventy to one hundred participants gathered at Big Beaver House Bible Camp. The trainers were Indigenous clergy and other diocesan personnel. This program was self-sufficient financially.

Three catechist's schools each attracted about one hundred and fifty men and women, and the communities that hosted these events paid part of the cost. Currently the program has two sessions a year. The first is a week in mid-February at the Mission House in Kingfisher Lake. The second is held at the Big Beaver House Bible Camp in the first two weeks of July, and many students bring their families. Most are fully employed in their communities, and so taking three weeks to attend TAIP is a major investment of time. Students are also expected to continue to study and be involved in their local parishes throughout the year. They are already active leaders in their community, the majority having long experience as lay readers.

The positive experience of TAIP also encouraged non-Indigenous congregations unable to support the ministry of full-time stipendiary clergy, to nurture persons in their own communities for leadership and ministry. Through a variety of approaches, these congregations have raised up a number of clergy.

In addition to training new clergy, TAIP provides ongoing learning opportunities for those who are already ordained. This program is run almost entirely by the Elders under the direction of Dr. William Winter, archdeacon emeritus.

Most of the teaching staff for TAIP are diocesan clergy, both seminary and non-seminary trained. However, the program also draws on national church staff, seminary professors, and members of the House of Bishops.

In 1999, the name of the program was changed from Train An Indian Priest to Train An Indigenous Priest.

Of necessity, TAIP has been a flexible program. Its very existence has resulted in the challenging of traditionally accepted ideas of the parish priest and parish ministry. It has meant that more and more ministry is derived from the local Christian community itself, with the work of the "official church" focused on training and equipping those chosen and called for ministry. It has caused us to look closely at what is required in ministry in our day, and to respond by finding a pragmatic way to meet the requirements.

Within the last few years there has been increased awareness of the negative effects of the government's official policy of assimilating First Nations peoples, and the focus has been on residential schools, which were the principal agents of assimilation. The discovery in the late 1980s that a well-respected priest had been sexually abusing young boys throughout the diocese has helped sensitize people to the problems of sexual abuse. The signing of The Covenant (an agreement to build a truly Anglican Indigenous Church in Canada), and a general reawakening of pride in First Nations culture and tradition, has helped us gain a new appreciation for the need to preserve and promote Indigenous languages. Consequently, while TAIP retains its basic structure of Old and New Testament study, church history, doctrine, liturgy, pastoral care, and parish organization, it is focusing much more energy on the ministry of clergy as healers and reconcilers in a broken hurting world. One thing that never changes, however, is the biblically based nature of the program. Worship and Bible study are essential elements. All teaching is supported by, and informed through, the scriptures.

Discussions are currently underway with chiefs and councils, Elders and clergy, educators and youth, and front line workers such as mental health and addictions counsellors to determine the ministry needs of the communities. Television and the Internet are both widely available in all communities. This exposure to "southern" culture threatens to undermine traditional teachings and to make language preservation and promotion much more difficult. Suicide, especially among young people, has become a very serious concern. Economic development is proceeding at a rapid rate. There are proposals to begin building all weather roads and power grids to most communities, which will not only end isolation but also introduce a whole new range of social problems. These emerging issues demand an immediate pastoral and prophetic response from the church.

TAIP is determined to remain faithful to its founding principles:

- to use progressive planning and a realistic approach to the needs of northern communities
- to consistently consult with, and respond to, the communities we serve
- to present new challenges and suggest new dimensions to the outreach work of the church in Canada
- to be a voice for First Nations people speaking out to the rest of the church

- to provide an opportunity for people outside our diocese to get involved in a project that has been long overdue in the church

TAIP has been very successful in providing a leadership role in the development and deployment of Indigenous clergy. More and more people, however, are coming forward from the communities to indicate that they want to receive theological training although they do not see themselves being ordained. There is an increased need for training from a biblical perspective in the areas of family life, addictions counselling, and political organization. TAIP will continue its tradition of consulting with local communities, researching resources, and developing training programs to equip the saints to fulfill their ministry in an era of rapid and radical change.

THE HENRY BUDD EXPERIENCE

Fletcher Stewart

Fletcher Stewart has been at the Henry Budd College for Ministry since 1991. He is the full-time principal in a team that includes one other part-time teacher and a part-time secretary-bookkeeper. Over his years there, he has found that an extension approach helps the curriculum to fit into people's lives. Funerals and wakes, for example, take up an important part in Indigenous communities, and the Theological Education by Extension (TEE) curriculum is flexible enough to work around these events and gatherings. Its focus is on community learning.

One after another, the candidates stood up at the lunch tables and expressed how much they had got from the assessment weekend. It had been an intense opportunity to think about one's life and ministry. One person summed it up: "I've never experienced so much growth all at once."

The assessment weekend was the high point to date in a program that trains local volunteer deacons to minister in their own communities in The Pas Deanery in northwestern Manitoba in the diocese of Brandon. Most of the students are taking their training through Henry Budd College for Ministry, based in The Pas.

The potential deacons are at various stages in their studies. Some have been training for many years for various forms of lay ministry. Others have more recently become students. All have been commended by their communities in consultation with their bishop and the college. The plan is to ordain them partway through their diaconal training so that they can learn "on the job."

This is an example of the growing practice of teaching by extension, increasingly being adopted in North America. In contrast to the traditional residential programs, the teachers or tutors go out to the communities, presenting evening courses to mature students. The curriculum that we are using at Henry Budd College for Ministry is based on one developed by Cook College and Theological School in Tempe, Arizona — pioneers in Theological Education by Extension in North America. Our emphasis is primarily on lay training. Candidates for ordained ministry emerge later.

TEE originated in developing countries in Latin America and Africa. Now we are finding it especially helpful in raising up Indigenous ministry among First Nations people. This is particularly significant as we follow The Covenant, and work towards an equal working relationship between Indigenous people and the rest of the Anglican Church of Canada.

This kind of approach is also used at the TEE Centre based in Terrace, BC. A number of dioceses are developing similar programs (for example, Moosonee, Saskatchewan). Vancouver School of Theology has also pioneered a TEE approach to deliver their Master of Divinity degree program in a culturally appropriate form to students preparing for Indigenous ministry. Somewhat different approaches are being used in the United and Roman Catholic churches. Even traditional residential colleges, such as Emmanuel and St. Chad in Saskatoon, are making special efforts to serve the needs of Indigenous students. There is a mood of cooperation and cross-fertilization between many of these programs. The Spirit is blowing through all the churches, and the historical moment seems right.

This is not the first moment in history when the attempt has been made to develop Indigenous ministry for First Nations communities. Back in 1840, when Henry Budd came as teacher and catechist to The Pas, the foundations were being laid. The strategy of the Church Missionary Society was to build up a self-propagating, self-governing, and self-supporting Indigenous church with its own Indigenous leadership. The members of the society believed that each nation should develop its own authentic embodiment of Christian faith and practice.

That policy was sidetracked by a century of colonial settlement. But training continued, especially for catechists, and there are notable examples of Indigenous priests who have helped to reshape the Anglican Church — Stan Cuthand and Andrew Ahenekew, for example. Following World War II, as Canada and the world grew out of the colonial mentality, the writing of missionaries such as Roland Allen became influential in creating a renewed interest in Indigenous models of ministry, and the Hendry Report impelled the Anglican Church of Canada to develop less paternalistic models of ministry in Indigenous communities.

At Henry Budd College for Ministry, we are training leaders for that Indigenous embodiment of the church on many levels, through a variety of courses and workshops. Much of our work is aimed at empowering a biblically and theologically literate laity to exercise their baptismal ministry in communities that are hurting from deep social problems and the disruption of their culture.

At more advanced levels, our training equips clergy who are locally raised up to administer word and sacraments to their own people, in both languages — English and Cree. Some go on to several years of further training towards the Master of Divinity degree from Vancouver School of Theology. The aim of our advanced levels of training is to produce a new generation of Indigenous clergy who will be able to take over training and supervisory tasks on an equal footing with their brothers and sisters of European ancestry.

It would be tempting to romanticize this approach. It is not free from problems. Students may be subject to unrealistic expectations, such as becoming brilliant preachers after a single course. It takes a long time to complete a program of study, taking only one course at a time. Teachers are spread thin, trying to meet so many needs in many different communities. Some natural leaders have been resistant to being taught and evaluated by outsiders and women.

One of the challenges of providing culturally sensitive education is that, while non-Indigenous people may be intent on changing colonial values, Indigenous people in a local context may cling to them. Traditional gender roles are a case in point. The Henry Budd College has regarded itself as a change agent for women's issues, and is intentional about creating a place and a space for women to support one another. The program has been cautious about "raising up natural leaders" in a context in which local communities may resist recognition of women or other outsiders. On the other hand, the best principles of Total Ministry are natural in Indigenous communities where lay readers, organists, prayer leaders, youth leaders, and musicians are identified by a community and accustomed to working together in a team.

Theological Education by Extension at the Henry Budd College offers two-credit courses in twelve sessions over three months. Weekend workshops at the centre are offered for credit. Students can take courses on Prayer Book studies, biblical studies, ethics and Christian life, theology and doctrine, church history, and pastoral skills, including helping others, crisis counselling, and pastoral theology. Students who have completed the program and have an interest in, and hunger for, further training are the ones who are likely to become candidates for ordination.

Other challenges too must be faced in the communities where trained people or people in training live and serve. Resistance may be offered to new approaches on issues ranging from using guitars in worship, to considering the use of some Indigenous ceremonies, to the remarriage of divorced people in the church, to healing from the effects of abuse. Expectations are often conditioned by the traditional role of white missionaries, particularly in administration and paperwork. Volunteer non-stipendiary clergy have found themselves burning out because of demands based on job descriptions appropriate to full-time clergy in a culture where it is difficult to say No.

It has proved difficult, because of family attachments, to place graduates in full-time positions away from their homes. Clan loyalties and personality conflicts have sometimes made it difficult for clergy to be fully accepted in their own communities. Health problems have taken a tragic toll among the clergy.

Despite these difficulties, there is a growing body of talented Indigenous people dedicated to training for a variety of ministries in service to their communities. There are no quick fixes, but there is steady growth.

THIRTY YEARS OF CHANGE AND DEVELOPMENT[5]

Caledonia

John A. (Ian) MacKenzie

On Sunday 4 January 1998, Bishop John Hannen licensed me as parish priest of Holy Trinity Church, New Aiyansh, British Columbia. The Rev. Percy Tait, the fourth Nisga'a clergyperson to be ordained in this Nisga'a community, had just retired. In some ways, I felt as if things had come full circle. After thirty years of working for the development of Indigenous ministry, establishing training programs, and participating in one way or another in twenty-two ordinations to the diaconate or priesthood of candidates selected and trained in their own congregations, we had hoped and expected that Percy would be succeeded by another Nisga'a clergyperson. That same afternoon, however, I participated in a meeting of twelve Nisga'a people gathered to explore the ministries to which God might be calling them.

---

5   This article is an edited and updated version of an essay first published in the summer edition of *Ministry Formation*, World Council of Churches (July 1999).

The diocese of Caledonia began working at alternate forms of ministry thirty years ago, when Bishop Munn proposed to a number of priests that ministry to the First Nations Anglican congregations on the north coast of British Columbia and the Nass Valley should be conducted by a community of clergy based in Port Edward. After several years, these itinerant priests concluded that, in order to provide effective ministry, a clergyperson needed to be resident in the villages for at least ten years.[6] By the late 1960s, it was apparent to these priests that within each village there were women and men who were the real ministers in the community.

Later, at several synods, Bishop Douglas Hambidge reminded the diocese that, in the history of Caledonia, only two candidates for ordination had emerged from congregations in the diocese. Priests came from elsewhere.[7] But during the early 1970s, it was becoming increasingly difficult to recruit people to live and work in the north. Also, northern dioceses were feeling economic pressures as the national church struggled to provide financial assistance. Bishop Hambidge challenged the diocese to consider prayerfully what we mean in our baptism when we are commissioned as ministers. He asked every member of the diocese to read one chapter of the Acts of the Apostles each day during a given month. At about the same time, he visited dioceses in Argentina and discovered the SEAN Bible study program (*Seminario por Extension A las Naciones*). He negotiated the right to translate this program into English and introduced it to the diocese in 1976.

---

6   As a result, John Blyth went to St. Peter's, New Aiyansh, David Retter to St. Andrew's, Greenville, and John Hannen to Christ Church, Kincolith.

7   The Rev. Paul Mercer was the first Nisga'a priest in the 1950s. Dr. Calder attended seminary in the early 1940s but on graduation was offered work as a deckhand on the mission boat by the bishop. He declined, and chose what came to be a spectacular political career, becoming the first Indigenous person within the British Commonwealth to be elected to a legislative assembly.

Within three years, over one thousand people in this small diocese were engaged in a program of Bible study that challenged its participants to consider their ministry and spawned a whole variety of lay ministries. By 1980, candidates for the permanent diaconate and the priesthood had emerged in both Indigenous and non-Indigenous congregations across the diocese.

While it was clear to most of us that this movement was led by the Holy Spirit, it was also evident that we needed to create a suitable training program for new forms of ministry. The story of transferring ordained ministry in Indigenous congregations from non-Indigenous clergy to First Nations clergy began in New Aiyansh.

When Hubert McMillan, a Nisga'a chief, was ordained to the diaconate and then to the priesthood, it was recognized that within First Nations communities there had been a long process of training for their religious leaders. The Church Army was a training ground. Lay readers had looked after Sunday services, funerals, and pastoral matters for most of the twentieth century in the absence of ordained clergy. But First Nations people themselves expected some kind of additional training and credentials. Perhaps eighty years of colonial experience had convinced them that seminary education and degrees were essential for a real clergyperson!

Shortly after I came to the diocese in 1975, Bishop Hambidge asked me to join some other diocesan clergy in attending a workshop at the College of Emmanuel and St. Chad in Saskatoon, led by resource people from Cook College and Theological School in Tempe, Arizona. The workshop introduced us to the current thinking about Theological Education by Extension (TEE) and the curriculum already available through Cook. By 1978, we had added to the SEAN program the Cook extension curriculum and had begun to send some of our ordination candidates to the Cook Winter School. The proposal to the 1979 synod that formally established the program in Caledonia explains the principles of TEE:

Theological Education by Extension (TEE) is a movement to renew the church by extending education to many community leaders instead of extracting a few people from communities for many years of schooling to become leaders. The TEE movement is based upon the conviction that (1) ministry belongs to all Christians and not just a few who can afford education; (2) the church can and should be indigenous; (3) a congregation has a right to self-determination, even if parish members are not wealthy; and (4) parishes have the right and the responsibility to participate in the selection of their own leaders instead of depending on outsiders for leadership. Educationally, TEE is based upon the belief that learning occurs best when (a) the study and practice of ministry are closely related; (b) people have the opportunity to study at their own pace and on their own level; and (c) innovative educational technology (such as programmed texts) is used widely.[8]

Almost immediately following this synod, Bishop Hambidge was transferred to the diocese of New Westminster, and in 1981, John Hannen was elected and consecrated Bishop of Caledonia. He asked me to become the archdeacon and to assume responsibility for training the candidates for ordination.

By 1983, twelve men and women were pursuing ordination to the diaconate or the priesthood. Ten were at the same time serving as partially or fully stipendiary ministers; the other two pursued their studies while working at full-time secular positions. We established a site in Terrace, with a full-time secretary,[9] as a resource

---

8   Presentation of Theological Education by Extension to the synod of the diocese of Caledonia, 1979.

9   Dorothy Smith was engaged for this position in 1987, and continues to do this job faithfully and well.

centre for congregations equipping the baptized for ministry, both lay and ordained. The bishop established a diploma to mark completion of the training process. To ensure exposure to other models of ministry and congregational life, all candidates were required to spend at least two weeks of training each year throughout their ministry in an environment outside of their own community.

A primary issue was accountability. Since the bishop shares authority with the local congregation in the selection of candidates for ordination, we expected that these congregations would also share the disciplinary side of the bishop's responsibility. We began to struggle with the problem of evaluating a minister's work in the context of a First Nations village, which is a community of relatives. How does the bishop share the exercise of discipline if the candidates engage in inappropriate behaviour? The congregations expected the bishop alone to demand accountability.

A major problem experienced in non-Indigenous congregations was the mobility of members. Some candidates preparing for priesthood would discover, four to five years later, that most of the congregation, many of whom were new, were not aware of this selection and did not always support it.

A Pacific Rim consultation on ministry held in Hawaii connected Caledonia First Nations people, Alaskan Indigenous people, and Maori from New Zealand. The bishops of Alaska and Caledonia asked me to set up a meeting with representatives of Vancouver School of Theology and Cook College and Theological School in order to explore ways to cooperatively establish TEE programs for this part of the Pacific Rim. If possible, we would also look for ways to include other Pacific Rim Indigenous groups in this endeavour.

These initiatives coincided with the challenge of First Nations Christians on the west coast of British Columbia who called upon the churches to establish new programs to equip Indigenous leaders for ordered and lay ministries in Indigenous congregations. The merging of these strands led to the creation of the Native

Ministries Consortium in 1985. The mandate of this First Nations controlled institution is:

- To refine and expand lay education in Indigenous villages on the west coast of Canada and Alaska;
- To develop an appropriate curriculum for Indigenous people entering the ordained ministry, with particular emphasis on the establishment of an extension or community based degree program;
- To establish appropriate cross-cultural courses to assist the church as a whole in its ministry with Indigenous peoples, with a particular attention to the infusion of Indigenous thought into the dominant society's Christian theological world;
- To commend to its founding institutions ways in which Indigenous people might gain a permanent and significant role and involvement in the educational decision making at all levels of the church and seminary.

The consortium has run summer schools every year since 1985, and has established these schools in cooperation with other institutions in South Dakota and Alaska. The school's student body and faculties have included people from New Zealand, Australia, Hawaii, Europe, Great Britain, Latin America, six Canadian provinces and the two territories, and at least ten US states, representing approximately twenty different First Nations.

The consortium began in 1986 to explore the possibility of Vancouver School of Theology (VST) offering a degree program for Indigenous ministries, both lay and ordained, because First Nations communities were insisting on a program that provided credentials equal to those of non-Indigenous ministers, while still taking into account the social, political, cultural, and religious traditions of each First Nation. VST accepted the idea of transforming their fully accredited Master of Divinity program into an extension program for delivery in the communities in which the candidates resided. Major grants came from the Trinity Grants program in New York City and the Maple Leaf Fund in Great Britain, and I was engaged as part-time director.[10] In this program, a student cannot simply apply to VST to enter the Native Ministries program by extension. The diocese, presbytery, or other ecclesiastical authority must apply on behalf of the student, and enter into a covenant relationship with VST under which the authority handles the cost of tutors, travel, and student expenses. Tutors are accredited by VST in partnership with the constituencies who put forward the student candidates.

A number of our potential candidates needed to acquire the equivalent of two years of college transfer credit.[11] The Native Ministries summer schools made this possible because their courses are recognized as college transfer credits. By 1996, our first students graduated. By 1998, the program was being delivered to thirty-two students in British Columbia, Saskatchewan, Alberta, Manitoba, Alaska, South Dakota, California, and Oregon. While most students and tutors are Anglican or Episcopalian, a growing number of participants are from the United Church of Canada and the Presbyterian Church in both Canada and the United States. About 70 per cent of the students are First Nations people.

---

10 The Rev. Pete Zimmer was appointed associate ministry development coordinator for the diocese, and became the first tutor in the VST extension program. He provided invaluable leadership in the formation of the extension curriculum. In 1994, the diocesan bishop appointed the Rev. Dr. John Mellis as the coordinator. He completed the tutoring and testing of the curriculum that resulted in the first three graduates of the extension program in 1996.

11 The Association of Theological Schools' current policy is that students can be admitted to the Master of Divinity degree program without a bachelor's degree if they have two years of college transfer credit, and can demonstrate the ability to complete master level work.

In 1997, an evaluation team from the Association of Theological Schools visited VST during the Native Ministries summer school, and recommended complete support and accreditation for this extension program. This decision was a significant breakthrough. Of primary importance is the acceptance of a new understanding of the "community of learning." Traditionally, it meant the residential community in a residential seminary. Now it includes the congregation, the community, and the socio-cultural environment in which the student is living, working, and learning. It also recognizes that the traditional library has been replaced by email, the Internet, fax machines, and good mail service. Yet extension programs are different from correspondence courses and other forms of distance learning because tutors are central to its success. These women and men work in a face to face relationship with the students, using a program prepared by VST faculty. Evaluations remain the responsibility of the faculty.

Following the 1998 celebration of the ministry of Percy Tait, the bishop began an intensive recruitment program with congregations in the diocese.[12] Now there are ten new First Nations deacons serving in four Indigenous congregations. There are two new priests and one deacon serving in non-Indigenous congregations, and one non-Indigenous priest who has completed the Master of Divinity by extension and serves in a First Nations congregation. Four of the new First Nations deacons are preparing for the priesthood through the Master of Divinity degree by extension. Four additional Indigenous lay persons are pursuing their call to ministry through the extension degree. One non-Indigenous priest is also enrolled in the extension degree, and the other priest is completing the bishop's diploma program.

In July 2000, the Rev. Dr. John Mellis of VST was appointed director of the VST Native Ministries program for a term of three

---

12   The Rev. Percy Tait passed away in January 1999.

years. The bishop initiated an evaluation of the Caledonia ministry development program, and the diocesan executive decided not to appoint a replacement to the ministry development staff position until this evaluation was completed. One reason to pause in the process is the uncertain financial situation of the diocese, along with all northern dioceses, because of the residential school suits against the Anglican Church of Canada, and the possible loss of grants from the national church for the operation of the diocese. (In 1999, the diocese of Caledonia received over $300,000 from the national church.) Another reason is the emergence of a desire on the part of some of the stipendiary seminary-educated priests and some laity to return to the traditional pattern of ministry. In their view, the funds used for training should be used for grants to parishes in order to provide full stipends to professional clergy, defined as residential seminary-educated clergy.

The bishop engaged Dr. Ross Kinsler to carry out the evaluation. He met with representatives of each region in the diocese and representatives of the Prince Rupert Presbytery.[13] Dr. Kinsler comments in his evaluation on the strength of the traditional model in light of the imminent retirement of Bishop Hannen and others who have been instrumental in developing these programs over the last thirty years in Caledonia and the Prince Rupert Presbytery:

> Education is commonly identified with schooling, which functions as a ladder that carries chosen individuals upward and onward towards professional qualification, power and privilege. It alienates the laity in virtually every field of competence, including the ministry, so that small and

---

13　The Presbytery joined the evaluation since much of the program is shared, e.g., the TEE Centre, the Native Ministries Consortium, and some course delivery.

remote communities and their natural leaders are increasingly disqualified and alienated from most of those fields.[14]

In the fall of 2000 and the spring of 2001, Dr. Kinsler's report was shared with the diocese for the purpose of developing a plan for the future of ministry in Caledonia. In March 2001, the executive of the diocese of Caledonia accepted a plan for the future and established the Caledonia School of Mutual Ministry (ww.geocities.com/calministry) as the succesor of the Ministry Development program.

. . .

After twenty-five years of working at these issues of alternative ministry and alternative training, what have I learned?

1. *The choice of alternative forms of ministry must be scripturally based.* The most successful developments in our diocese have emerged from congregations where there has been serious Bible study. It is my firmly held belief that while economic, social, and other factors may be part of the impetus for change, these alternative programs must also be rooted in the study of the Bible or they will eventually fail.

2. *The selection process is crucial.* Despite lots of training and education, mature adults largely have been formed before they enter the training process. Our expectation of their abilities and performance needs to recognize that, although they will improve their skills, discover their gifts, and increase their knowledge, they will not change much through our training. This means that careful selection is of the first importance.

---

14 F. Ross Kinsler, "The Ministry Development Program of the Diocese of Caledonia and Prince Rupert Presbytery at the Dawn of the New Millennium," report to the diocese of Caledonia, 1999, p. 5.

3. *Stable congregational communities are essential.* In Indigenous congregations, there is a permanent closely knit congregation and community of large extended families. These are communities who know who they are. But urban and even many rural congregations are characterized by rapid change in membership and continuing struggles to recreate community. While Indigenous communities provide their own problems for congregations, the constant change in non-Indigenous congregations may be a serious problem for the permanency of many of the current non-traditional models of ministry.

4. *The alternative ministry vision must be constantly reinterpreted and reinforced.* A major challenge where Mutual Ministry becomes the model is continual education of the members of the congregation. While a core group of people may be familiar with the vision and well versed in the process, ministers meet daily demands for service by those who know only the traditional model. On the other hand, where Mutual Ministry is operating and an ordained person brought up and following the traditional model is asked to minister, the problem is reversed. The issue then is for the ordained outsider to make sure he or she does not get in the way of the ministries being exercised by the laity in that congregation.

5. *Accountability and evaluation processes are incomplete and still evolving.* One of the most difficult issues for First Nations congregations and their ecclesiastical authorities is the question of discipline and accountability. While First Nations congregations have played a significant part in the selection of candidates, they have not been able to develop accountability practices to deal with concerns about their own ministers. They are not alone. Very few parishes, Indigenous or non-Indigenous, have figured out good evaluation procedures for their own lay and ordained ministries, nor have dioceses for the evaluation of bishops. For tribal communities and congregations, however, a culturally appropriate evaluation

methodology has not emerged. This is true for most tribal institutions, not just the church.

6. *Coordination, supervision, and interaction will always be required.* When in 1974–75 we began to discuss the possibility of some members of the Haida congregation on the Queen Charlotte Islands becoming deacons and priests, Bishop Hambidge made clear to the Haida that such a move did not mean that the diocese would cease to support them. As more and more congregations in Caledonia opted for this emerging form of Mutual Ministry, however, and as our professional resources diminished, it became very difficult to provide adequate support. In many cases, the result was the dwindling of the development in the congregations. Mutual ministry needs significant and permanent supervision and interaction from outside the congregation, as well as within it.

7. *The traditional model is very difficult to change.* I think the most significant learning for me is the terrifying recognition of the depth and strength of the professional, hierarchical, and male model of ministry. This means that current alternative models need to push hard to survive. Perhaps, until the whole church radically changes, all of our efforts to implement what we believe to be the biblical model will fail. This is more than a political issue. Rather, the existing traditional model appears to be rooted in the very being of the Anglican Church, and deeply branded on each individual Anglican worshipper's psyche.

Institutions have such a strong internal socialization and assimilative nature, that it may be better and more culturally appropriate for some groups, such as First Nations, to receive equal credentials through extension.

The rapid changes coming into play through computers and electronic communication as we enter the second millennium pose a major challenge to all education theory and methods, and particularly challenge the churches. Our churches are slow to keep abreast of changes in the human and physical environment in which we live.

The Native Ministries program, the Native Ministries Consortium, and Vancouver School of Theology, funded by the Trinity Grants program, hosted a global consultation, "TEE and Technology," in May 1997. This consultation posited a number of recommendations. One important conclusion was that the two methods of education complement each other. To put it another way, the future of both ministry and training/education for ministry rests with those residential programs that will take seriously the community of learning provided by the local communities and congregations, and make use of the modern tools of communication to connect the seminary to the local community.[15]

In my opinion, the last thirty years in Caledonia have demonstrated that TEE does offer new possibilities for ministry, and it has opened doors for many women and men previously excluded from ministry. This has been particularly the case for First Nations people in this diocese. TEE has also made possible the continued provision of ordained and lay ministries to many communities that otherwise would have been deprived of them. All of this has resulted in a sustained and strong ministry of the whole people of God.

---

15 The TEENET website has been established at www.teenet.net. The full report may be read there as well as information about the TEE programs.

A THEOLOGY
OF MINISTRY

THE BREAD WILL RISE

The Distinctive Calling
of the Laity

Maylanne Maybee

THE BEGINNINGS OF BAPTISMAL MINISTRY

On 6 January, the Feast of the Epiphany, six-year-old Matthew was baptized with his eight-year-old brother, and the two of them received communion for the first time. The next day, Matthew's grade one teacher asked his students to draw a picture of something they had done over the Christmas holidays.

The following Sunday, Matthew showed me what he had drawn: a font, a stool, and a small boy standing next to a jug of water. The boy's head was a circle, and if you looked closely, you could see that a cross had been crayoned in yellow, filling the circle, covering the whole head. Under the picture, in huge childish letters, were the words: "I GOT BAPTIZED."

His baptism was the high point of his Christmas holidays, indeed of his whole life. His grasp of its meaning was simple and deep: he belonged to Christ.

Stephanie, a medical lab technician, was baptized at the Easter Vigil. The bishop was present, and poured three jugs full of water over her head. We had made careful preparations for this form of baptism — setting up a small wading pool for her to stand in, warming up tubs of water, having lots of towels on hand, providing a screen behind which she could change. None of us, however, were prepared for her reaction, and ours, at the moment of baptism: pure, joyful, life-giving laughter!

Robert was baptized by immersion, also at an Easter Vigil. The server, a fourteen-year-old boy who was losing interest in matters relating to God and the church, watched as Robert, dressed in shorts and T-shirt, climbed into the font (a horse trough, bought for the occasion), knelt down, and allowed the priest to immerse him three times. Our best efforts to heat up pots and kettles of water made little difference to the temperature of the water. Robert's eyes filled with tears, as much from the cold as from the emotion of the moment. But if you looked closely, you could see that the server's eyes had filled with tears too. He later told me that, in spite of horse trough and cold water, he was moved by the unexpected dignity of the occasion.

Each person had a deeper story to tell. Matthew had been born within a year after his mother and father, thinking they would never become biological parents, had adopted his older brother. His brother had recently been diagnosed with a serious childhood disease; his mother had joined a twelve step program. The whole family had found support from the church at these critical moments, and were taking steps to deepen their involvement.

Stephanie had been abused by an older relative in her childhood. In adulthood she had abandoned whatever religious affiliation she had once had. Her faith, however, had not abandoned her, and she courageously embarked on a journey of therapy and healing. Through a friend at work, she started going to church again and decided it was time to make a full commitment.

Robert, a teacher of English at a community college, had never been baptized. He had been raised in a church with a strict and rigid view of the world, and wanted nothing to do with religion in his adulthood, even after marrying a woman deeply involved in the Christian life, and having children who were baptized and raised in the church. Over the years he realized, through the gentle influence of his family, that he was truly a follower of Christ at heart, and that he was finally ready to acknowledge this formally by full immersion baptism (his own request.)

Matthew, Stephanie, and Robert, though at very different points in their life journey, had each encountered God in some way — through a healing relationship, through crisis and change, through finding maturity and forgiveness. Their initial encounter with God may have been deeply personal, private, or solitary, but their baptism marked a turning point, for they were now ready to join themselves to a community of faith. With the encouragement of a friend, partner, parent, or other family member, they were introduced and admitted with due ceremony into the faith, traditions, and fellowship of the church.

Things happened very differently when my brother was baptized in the early 1950s. I was five years old, he a newborn infant. My mother dressed him in a long white baptismal gown ("This is probably the only time you'll ever wear a dress!" said my father.) It was a Saturday afternoon — the event timed so that there could be a family reception in the evening. A handful of friends and relatives assembled at the back of our little church. When I asked, I was told that a couple of out of town guests whom I didn't recognize would be my brother's godparents. The service unfolded — a series of phrases read from a book alternately by the congregation and minister, a man vested in cassock, surplice, and preaching scarf. The font, which looked to me like a basin on a pedestal, had been uncovered and filled with water. When the moment came to touch my brother's forehead with water, I'm told I said quite loudly: "Mind you don't get his pretty dress all wet!" I'm sure the service lasted no more than twenty minutes.

Compare this to the description of a baptismal rite in the late second or early third century. Those presenting themselves for baptism were assumed to be adults. They had to go through a rigorous admission process to ensure that they were living a life befitting a new Christian. They had to spend up to three years in instruction and prayer. They were scrutinized to see whether they were appropriately engaged in good works. As the date of baptism approached, they received the rite of exorcism with daily laying on hands. On the Saturday before Easter, they met with their bishop, received a final rite of exorcism, and spent the night in prayerful vigil. At dawn, they were taken to the baptistry, an enclosed room with a small pool, where they removed all clothing and jewellery. The bishop was present, accompanied by presbyters and deacons. As the candidates descended one by one into the font, a presbyter would ask whether they believed in the Father, then the Son, then the Holy Spirit in the Holy Church. Each time, the reply would be, "I believe! " The deacon, already in the water, would then immerse the candidates, three times in all. After that, they would ascend and receive the oil of thanksgiving, before drying off, dressing, and taking their place in the eucharistic assembly, led by the bishop. Here, the bishop would lay on hands and invoke the Holy Spirit, make the sign of the cross with oil, and say, "I anoint thee with holy oil in God the Father Almighty and Christ Jesus and the Holy Ghost."[16]

Times have changed. As the boundary shifts between church and world, baptism is shifting too, from being a private naming ceremony to a major rite of initiation. With some abridgments and informalities, the forms of baptism for Matthew, Stephanie, and Robert look more like what happened in the earlier church than what happened at my brother's baptism. None of the candidates was an infant. For each of them, baptism marked a turning point in their lives, a moment of conversion or transformation for themselves and their families. The services all took place within the eucharist, in the midst of the whole congregation, at the Easter

---

16   See Aidan Kavanaugh, *The Shape of Baptism: The Rite of Christian Initiation* (New York: Pueblo Publishing Co. Inc., 1978), p. 54ff. See also William H. Willimon, *Remember Who You Are: Baptism, a Model for Christian Life* (Nashville: Upper Room Books, 1980), p. 5ff.

Vigil or another major feast day of the church. For two of the candidates, there was much more water than a mere dribble on the forehead. Even if the bishop was not personally present, the candidates were anointed with oil that had been blessed by the bishop. Some candidates had gone through a significant period of preparation with other "catechumens"— they had met throughout Lent for learning, study, and prayer; they had spent an evening with the bishop; they had visited diocesan ministries with people suffering from poverty, imprisonment, or illness.

THE DIMENSIONS OF BAPTISMAL MINISTRY

Like Matthew, our church is beginning to realize that being baptized is a pretty big deal. We're starting to articulate a theology of "baptismal ministry" that's big enough for all God's people, recognizing that baptism gives every Christian a part in the church's life and mission, a purpose in life, and a new relationship with God and other human beings.

Being baptized means we renounce evil and turn our attention to God. Having made a leap of faith to believing that God is present in a world where we know there is evil and violence and death, we allow ourselves to be immersed into a life that is grounded in creativity, reconciliation, and giftedness. In the waters of baptism, we embrace God's very way of being, a unity that is egalitarian and profoundly mutual, at once deeply personal and in sustained relationship with others. "The vocation of every baptized person," says William Stringfellow, "is to live from day to day, whatever the day brings, in this extraordinary unity, in this reconciliation of all people and all things, in this knowledge that death has no more power, in this truth of resurrection."[17]

---

17   William Stringfellow, *Instead of Death* (New York: The Seabury Press, 1963), p. 112.

At baptism, we publicly confess our belief in the Trinity. We accept the faith of the apostles who first witnessed the One who lived and died and rose from the dead. We vow to continue in the tradition and fellowship of the apostles, "in the breaking of bread and in the prayers," and to proclaim by word and example the good news of God in Christ. We call our church *apostolic* because its people are sent with authority to proclaim the gospel.

Baptism also admits one into Christ's *priesthood.* We have been conditioned to think that priesthood is conferred at ordination, but fundamentally it is an attribute of Christ that is most clearly seen when it is enacted corporately, by all the members of the body. "Christians do not ordain to priesthood," says Aidan Kavanaugh, "they baptize to it.... Priesthood comes upon one in baptism, and thus *laos* is a priestly term for a priestly person. The vocabulary of priestliness, with which Christian tradition is ingrained, denotes a *christic*, i.e., a messianic-sacerdotal-royal, quality which all the baptized share in the Anointed One himself."[18]

At baptism, we vow to continue to struggle against and resist evil, and when we sin, to repent and continually turn our lives over to God. We become part of a community that blesses and makes holy the ordinary things of creation through offering and thanksgiving — bread and wine, money and labour, sex and babies, poetry and music, our very selves. We undertake to live in communion with one another, to face and transcend our diversity, to forgive one another, to heal conflicts and resolve differences. Holiness, blessing, reconciliation, forgiveness, the power to offer sacrifice — these are qualities of priesthood, and they are the functions of baptismal ministry.

Ministry in and for the world has a name too: *diakonia.* As with priesthood, we have been conditioned to think of *diakonia* as an attribute of the ordained. But at root, *diakonia* — "servant ministry"

---

18 *Anglican Theological Review* 66, no. 1 (Supplementary Series 9; 1984): 40.

or simply "service" — is a characteristic of Christ, whose own life set an unprecedented example of what it could mean. Of the four gospels, John's especially emphasizes the diaconal relationship between Jesus and God, his "abba." Jesus speaks of himself as God's agent and entrusted messenger. He claims that he did not come on his own but was authorized by "the Father." Yet he exercised this divine authority by mingling with outcasts and sinners, ministering to the poor and the oppressed, washing the feet of his disciples.

At baptism, we take on this same diaconal relationship. We vow to seek and serve Christ in all persons, to strive for justice and peace among all people, to respect the dignity of every human being. As a diaconal people, we are dismissed from the altar into our daily lives to be ambassadors of Christ, to mend what is wrong, to love God's world.

If we really believe what we say and do at baptism, then every Christian stands within the apostolic tradition of the early church. Every Christian is imprinted with and contains the priestly and diaconal character of Christ, the way an amoeba contains within itself the life forms of creation. Priesthood and *diakonia* are not superadded at ordination; they are given at baptism.

BAPTISM AND MEMBERSHIP IN THE CHURCH

We learn our baptismal ministry through liturgy, which means "work for the people." The Orthodox have a saying that when the Sunday liturgy is over, the weekday liturgy — the liturgy of our lives — begins. For liturgy in its true sense is much more than "the work of the people who go to church": it is a public work accomplished not for ourselves only, but for people who inhabit the world — the people we encounter in our household, workplace, marketplace, and neighbourhood. Walter Brueggemann, in his book *Israel's Praise*, describes liturgy as remembering, enacting, and hoping for liberation. Liturgy is not secret or private, not about escaping or withdrawing from the world; rather, it is about "world making" — shaping our worldview into God's.[19] Ultimately, it is about *living our lives,* and it applies to all of God's people, every one, apart and together, gathered and scattered.

This has important implications for our ecclesiology, that is, how we understand the church. When we are baptized, we are made part of a living body, which Paul describes quite literally as the physical body of Christ. In 1 Corinthians he enjoins the community of the faithful not to be identified with any one part of the body. In fact, he says, it is precisely those parts of the body that seem to be weakest that are indispensable! "Now you are the body of Christ and individually members of it." This means that the church is a community with not just one but many centres of giftedness and leadership, and that no one person can function in isolation from the whole. It suggests a radical mutuality in which members of the church apprehend God not just through the ordained but also through each other, and through all the other members of the church.

It also suggests that the body of the church, like the body of Christ, is given to the whole world. Wes Frensdorff, the late bishop of Nevada and an early protagonist of Total Ministry, suggested that we imagine the local unit of church, the congregation, as an ellipse, organized around two focal points. One focal point represents the life of the church as it gathers for worship, learning, and fellowship; the other represents the church in mission as it disperses for service and action beyond itself. There is interplay between these aspects, but one is not more important than the other, nor is one complete without the other.[20]

---

19   Walter Brueggemann, *Israel's Praise: Doxology against Idolatry and Ideology* (Philadelphia: Fortress, 1988), p. 6.

20   See Wesley Frensdorff, "Ministry and Orders: A Tangled Skein," in *Reshaping Ministry: Essays in Memory of Wesley Frensdorff,* edited by Josephine Borgeson and Lynne Wilson (Arvada, Colorado: Jethro Publications, 1990).

THE ECCLESIAL MINISTRY OF THE BAPTIZED, BASED IN THE GATHERED LIFE OF THE CHURCH

What the laity already do in their own right expresses their baptismal identity in its many dimensions. One dimension is *ecclesial*— that is, based in the gathered life of the church, where the laity enact their priesthood in several specific ways:

1. *By coming together for solemn assembly, Sunday by Sunday, feast days and holidays, intentionally and regularly.* Simply to gather for anything other than sports or entertainment is a profoundly counter-cultural act, especially in a society where our lives are both fragmented and separated from each other. Sports and school events that last late into the evenings and take up both weekend days, summer homes and holidays away from home, business travel, and work itself — all contrive to keep us apart. We are conditioned to live in separate and private cocoons, to be independent and self-sufficient, and to assemble only as consumers and spectators. Coming together to break bread is the first priestly act of the laity.

2. *By praying.* I once heard it suggested that simply belonging to and participating in a community of prayer would contribute more than any demonstration, petition, letter, or speech, to the balance, peace, and transformation of the world. That is what God does in Christ, and it is what God's people do in the church. In baptism, we take on Christ and commit ourselves to wear Christ over and over, in eucharist, in prayer, in the reading of scripture, until there is no difference between garment and skin.

3. *By "owning" the liturgy — making it our business to know what's going on, and to participate in the movement of worship.* A mature and robust laity do not depend passively on instruction from a person or a book, but form a deep relationship with the liturgy and with one another. For it is the whole assembly, the *laos*, who are the celebrants and subjects of the eucharistic prayer. In a similar way,

the members of an orchestra or choir work together, observant of a conductor's direction but equally attentive to their own and others' voices or instruments, and guided by a disciplined sense of the music itself. Patterns of worship that encourage passivity, where only one person knows what's going on and does everything, or that rely heavily or exclusively on printed text, do not help to form a priestly people.

4. *By actively participating in liturgy and community, the contexts in which we grow into our priesthood.* As we learn to pray and sing and do ritual together, the liturgy, as Thomas Merton says, enters the bones and we become transformed by it. I see this in my parish church when parishioners come to church daily to prepare for and participate in Holy Week — a participation that engages the mind, the senses, and the heart. They rehearse music, trim candles, bake hot cross buns, compose prayers, and press linen. They process with palms, recite the passion narrative, remove socks and shoes, pour water and dry it off, scrub the altar, extinguish and light candles, get splashed with water. These subtle processes of cooperation, interaction, offering and receiving gifts, sharing and rotating roles are both an expression and a formation of our priesthood.

5. *By singing.* Choral singing itself is a quintessentially priestly function. I can't think of anything else this side of heaven that more closely expresses priestly creativity, singularity-within-unity, self-offering, and power to transform than a community of people who sing in harmony with one another. Hans Ruedi-Weber, formerly director of biblical studies at the World Council of Churches, says that "singing is the way in which theology is communicated in that particular part of the New Testament."[21] Chanting and singing are,

---

21 Hans Ruedi-Weber, *Living in the Image of Christ* (Geneva: WCC Publications; Pennsylvania: Judson Press:, 1986), p. 65.

in fact, one of the oldest ways of memorizing and communicating biblical stories and affirmations of faith. For this reason, I believe that singing the liturgy is preferable to saying it, and having the whole congregation sing is preferable to a choir.

6. *By being in communion and community with one another.* Priesthood is not only ceremonial and symbolic, although it is at least those things. It is also opening oneself to others. A full-blooded laity are aware of their shared pastoral role in creating a priestly community, which by nature is radically inclusive and uniting. They keep the boundaries of their communities open, break down divisions, and gather others in. They learn and know how to make and be disciples; how to nurture diversity; how to respect, love, and be changed by the other; how to live with difficult people (oneself included!), accept differences, and get through situations of conflict. They understand and practise the complex processes of forgiveness, restitution, and reconciliation.

To summarize these points: the laity express their priesthood by gathering, praying and singing together, organizing and taking meaningful part in worship, building up strong Christian communities, welcoming strangers and newcomers, relating to unlike (and sometimes difficult) people, handling conflict, teaching and learning.

A healthy church is one in which these responsibilities are neither dumped on nor hoarded by the ordained leadership, nor are they meted out in token spoonfuls to the laity. Thus we need to add one more point to this description of the ecclesial dimension of baptismal ministry.

7. *By enacting their priesthood through selecting ordained leadership, working out a relationship with that person or persons, and holding each other mutually accountable in that shared role, as peers and equals.* Priesthood is corporately shared among people and clergy, and is something that one grows into over time. This relationship is complex

and subtle, perhaps not unlike a marriage, except that because many more people are involved, there are many more variables.

The complicated interplay between lay leadership and ordained leadership

A booklet written in the 1970s and published by the Alban Institute gives an account of how the people of St. Mark's, Capitol Hill, in Washington, DC, prepared for and managed to survive a six-month period without their rector, who was taking a sabbatical away from the parish.[22]

Reading the booklet makes me smile a bit. They spared no expense in hiring consultants, professional counsellors, and supply clergy to fill in the gaps, and received almost weekly correspondence from their absent rector. I guess it was pretty big stuff in those days for a church to function without its resident priest. The study is nevertheless useful for pointing out what is at issue when God's people set about doing God's work "from scratch."

In preparing for their rector's departure, the parish had to look at all that is involved in leading and living their gathered life — managing, administering, and facilitating decisions; building relationships and coping with conflict; maintaining buildings; planning programs; teaching children, youth, and adults about the faith and about the how-to's of ministry; prayer, Bible study, counselling, visiting the sick, bringing communion to the shut in, conducting funerals, and comforting the bereaved. They began to realize that none of these tasks *have* to be done by clergy, but that they had come to expect that they would.

They did not touch the whole area of what is involved in leading worship, especially the eucharist. If they had, they might have

---

22 James R. Adams and Celia A. Hahn, *Learning to Share the Ministry* (Washington, DC: Alban Institute, 1975).

realized that it is relatively easy to learn what is necessary to lead worship — when to sit and when to stand, what to say in prayers and sermons and how to say it, where to look and in what book for lessons, psalms, and so on, what hymns to pick. Some people who have confidence, a good singing voice, a public presence, or a smooth tongue may have more of a knack at doing these things than others, and some people may feel discomfort or a sense of impropriety in performing some of these roles unless they have been given a "proper" education, license, or authority.

But there is something still more complex at issue. An interesting finding in the study of St. Mark's, Capitol Hill, is that something in a community wants a person or persons to represent them and speak for them. When that space is vacant, there is a lot of discussion about who has the authority and the credentials to fill it.

Interestingly, it is these very discussions that help to form Christian community and priestly identity. They force us to ask: What kind of people are we? What kind of leadership do we want? Who do we want to represent us, to speak for us, to show us and others what kind of people we are? John Zizioulas, an Orthodox theologian, has made the fascinating argument that ordination (that is, assignment to a particular *ordo* in the community) appears paradoxically not to follow from a pre-existing community but to *constitute* community.[23] Perhaps this is why Total Ministry congregations, who work so hard at discerning, negotiating, and assigning roles, have become so vitalized. By contrast, the usual church politics of selection and appointment, which are so consistently divorced from the politics of the community where the ordained person will serve, are often injurious to the priestly formation of the laity.

---

23   John D. Zizioulas, *Being as Communion: Studies in Personhood and the Church* (New York: St. Vladimir's Seminary Press, 1985).

The diaconal ministry of the baptized

The diaconal ministry of the laity takes place both within and beyond the church. Compassion for others based on love is as vital a tradition of the church as service at the altar. Services of compassion are not limited to the Christian community, but extend towards those who are afflicted or in need wherever they are found. Just as Jesus' deeds were signs of salvation to those at the edge of human existence, so true service is extended to the endangered edges of society — "outside the gate," which is where Christ suffered.

This ministry is especially important in a society where service has become professionalized, with the result that individuals are made to feel helpless or not responsible for the well-being of others or even themselves. The most effective way the church can express the love of Christ is to gather those who are ready to assist the isolated and the vulnerable, and equip them for service. For this purpose, the church needs leadership based on an understanding of Christ as High Priest and Servant. It needs preaching and teaching that enjoins people to service without being cynical about the world or making formless unrealistic calls for help, without saying who is to be helped, or where, or how.

Natural and neighbourly church based service gives members of the local congregation a specific sense of direction and obligation, and at the same time offers personal as well as professional institutional care to the lonely and the afflicted. Public social services can rarely compensate for the dissolution of families or create situations in which people care for each other. As a result, the old, the sick, the disabled, and the young may suddenly be left helpless and in danger, simply because they have no one who cares for them. We need communities that will keep those at risk in their accustomed surroundings, and only in extreme cases transplant them into specialized environments.

For eight months I was in charge of an inner city parish that included a mental health centre. One of our parishioners, an elderly woman living alone and in some degree of crisis, was admitted into the geriatric ward for assessment and stabilization. She was never released, even following a court hearing in which she begged to be sent home. The woman lived around the corner from the church that she had attended all her life, and was known to every parishioner. I brought her communion every week, but my time was limited and my responsibilities were essentially presbyteral, so I could not organize the volunteer care that would be necessary if she moved back home. She died in hospital soon after I left the parish, but to this day I am convinced that, had I been free to function as a deacon and to give leadership to the service of the laity, it would have been possible for her to live and die in the familiar surroundings of her neighbourhood and church community.

There are many emphases for present day *diakonia*: affirming family life, supporting parents of small or handicapped children, giving care and service to the sick in mind and body, attending to the elderly, the young, and those diagnosed with psychiatric disorders. At a recent conference for people involved in food ministries, we talked about "the downstairs church" — the food pantries, thrift shops, AA groups, child care programs, and drop-in centres — where much of the church's diaconal ministry takes place. Many of our churches have formal or informal "cells" or "mission groups" that draw together people who feel a special calling to "downstairs ministry" or some other form of pastoral care, social service, or public advocacy. In these and many other ways, Christians already offer the servanthood of Christ. We live in a time when the world more than ever needs people who give rather than grasp, who listen rather than tell, who serve rather than rule.

THE CONTEXT FOR BAPTISMAL MINISTRY

The primary locale where the *laos* live out their baptism is in their households, workplaces, neighbourhoods, schools, and marketplaces. The church's dispersed ministry does not happen in church. It is not done primarily by the ordained. It requires competency, relationship skills, good stewardship, sound ethics, the ability to navigate through change, and a strong sense of Christian values.

The church, however, tends to focus its resources and attention on the performance of ministry *inside* its boundaries. Although we use phrases such as "lay ministry" or "baptismal ministry" to emphasize that all Christians have an important role, we have yet to learn how to direct our resources and attention to the performance of ministry outside the church. What would help to support the church's scattered ministry?

The most important activities the church can do differently are

1. to equip the laity to discover their vocation in the world,
2. to nurture a spirituality that works in the world.

These would be major correctives to a church that tends to shore up its institutional boundaries, to be preoccupied with organizational self-preservation, and to direct its resources — financial and spiritual — to its own hierarchy.

Understanding and supporting the nature of *call* is the job of the church. Sadly, for too long this understanding has been narrowly focused on ordination. My own memory of "vocation Sunday," when I was a girl, was a pep rally for young men to consider studying for the priesthood. Fortunately, the church is beginning to realize that it cannot continue with such a blinkered worldview. We are learning that the needs of both current members and seekers demand a deeper and much more sophisticated understanding of what people yearn for and how they can be supported.

Michael Thompson and Paul MacLean, in their book *Seeking the Seekers*, describe a project in which they convened several focus groups of non-churchgoing people to listen and learn what kept them out of the church. Among their findings was that people outside the church long for a sense of identity, a sense of vocation, a reaffirmed sense of "adult life competence," and the opportunity for new insights and expanded self-understanding.

They long for these things but do not see the church as a place where they will find them.

> The need for a life following a vocation and lived with passion emerged as an affirmation of passionate personal engagement with the challenges and beauties of life. But it also emerged as a critical reflection on the absence of passion and the absence of encouragement for people's passionate living in the institutional church.[24]

Richard Bolles is a pioneer in encouraging people's search for vocation and passionate engagement with the world. He started out as an Episcopalian priest, but since 1972 has researched, written, edited, and updated the quintessential guide to lay ministry, *What Color Is Your Parachute?* In the pink pages at the end of each year's edition, he has a section on "How to Find Your Mission in Life." In those pages, he describes the discernment of personal mission on three levels:

1. *the level of standing in the conscious presence of God*, the one from whom we came and to whom we shall return;
2. *the level of decision making*, those little and big moments when we can choose to make a difference in the world around us;
3. *the level that is specific and personal* — the use of our greatest gifts in the place to which one is most drawn for the purpose that God most deeply desires.

---

24 Paul MacLean and Michael Thompson, *Seeking the Seekers: Serving the Hidden Spiritual Quest* (Toronto: Anglican Book Centre Publishing, 1999), p. 98.

Bolles quotes these words of Frederick Buechner: "The place where God calls you to is the place where your deep gladness and the world's deep hunger meet."[25]

The world's deep hunger is the reason that God pitched a tent and lived among us. And the world's deep hunger is the ultimate reason for lay ministry and liturgy — both are the work of God's people. It is a hunger that is the same yet radically different in every age. The world's deep hunger in our age is for a spirituality — a vision of holiness — that opens new spaces, that works for a global community, that recognizes modern day saints of any religion who inspire and exemplify good news to the captives and liberation to the oppressed, that offers hope for an end to violence, and that supplies grace in the face of the defilement of daily living: global warming, ecological collapse, AIDS, carcinogenic food, water that is poisonous and commodified.

DECLERICALIZING THE CHURCH: SUPPORTING THE *LAOS* IN THEIR MINISTRY IN THE WORLD

God's people are called to find their deep joy where there is deep hunger in the world. It is outrageous — blasphemous, in fact — to imagine that this calling would be confined only to the ordained, or to think that its fulfilment would be for the benefit of only the baptized. In John's account of the cleansing of the temple, Jesus' anger against the moneychangers was not because they had chosen an inappropriate venue for their trade, but because they had turned the temple that represented God's desire for humankind

---

25 Richard Nelson Bolles, *What Color Is Your Parachute? A Practical Manual for Job-Hunters and Career-Changers* (Berkeley, California: Ten Speed Press, 1994 edition), pp. 443–449.

into a means to pursue their own selfish and self-enclosed interests. Later Stephen, the deacon and martyr, angered the elders of the temple by stating with bold zeal and utter intransigence that the temple itself was no longer significant in the greater scheme of God's relationship with the world because all the earth was God's footstool.

Somehow the church has got itself into a similar mess. It has developed a clerical class who act as gatekeepers, securing the treasures of the church from the rest of humankind, and a laity who are regarded as passive dependants. Yet it is only through lay perspective and expertise that the church can minister to the whole suffering world. How do we solve the problem?

1. *We need a heightened view of the baptismal authority of all God's people.* This means blurring the sometimes rigid line that is drawn between the ordained and ordinary Christians. In a recent article on authority in the church, Fredrica Harris Thompsett, a professor of theology at the Episcopal Divinity School in Cambridge, Massachusetts, proposed that "we suspend using the adjective 'lay' to describe any group of Christians."[26] Its only use is to belittle those who are not ordained and to separate the church's common ministry and mission into professional and non-professional components. Why, she asks, do we constantly have to insert the word "lay" in front of functions and tasks exercised by many Christians — lay reader, lay leader, lay pastoral worker, lay theologian? "I prefer to speak instead," she continues, "of the ministry of all the baptized, the high calling of the baptized, and the authority of the baptized."[27]

---

26   Fredrica Harris Thompsett, "Authority Begins at Baptism," in *The Witness* (March 2000): 15.

27   *Ibid.*

2. *Conversely, we need a somewhat humbler view of the authority —
and capacity — of the ordained.* We overload them with tasks and
expectations that belong to the entire body: visiting the sick; counselling; making major financial decisions; quelling arguments;
attending every meeting in the parish and presiding over most;
supervising staff and volunteers; being a major discerner of gifts;
being the congregation's primary or only catechist, teacher,
evangelizer and greeter; getting along with absolutely everyone;
appealing to children, youth, parents, and the elderly; representing the parish on all civic and social occasions.

This misses the point that the real reason the church ordains
people is to give them a certain seat or role in the liturgy. We often
joke that priests work only one day a week — and if they were
limited to presiding, hearing confessions, blessing oil, baptizing in
the bishop's absence, and occasionally preaching, that would con-
ceivably be true. The rest of the week, clergy live out their baptismal
ministry just as other Christians do, and with a status no different
from that of other Christians.

3. *We need to find new ways and opportunities to forge a healthy relationship between the whole people of God and the church's ordained
leadership.* If what happens at ordination forms community and
shapes the identity of the *laos* (the whole people of God), then
ordination sermons, for example, should not be addressed to or
speak about the candidates alone. At such moments, we all need to
be reminded of how priesthood informs our daily lives; how *diakonia*
applies in our home or workplace; or how we share in the episcopal ministry of oversight, teaching, and unity whenever we chair
meetings, raise our children in the faith, or cooperate with fellow
Christians. Unfortunately, our services of ordination and induction are all too often triumphal occasions that elevate the clergy,
exclude the rest of the baptized, and send the unmistakable message that there is only one kind of ministry in the church that
counts.

4. *We can stop regarding the laity as a fourth order, non-ordained and non-professional.* The laity are already fully authorized and empowered by baptism to proclaim the apostolic faith, to partake in priestly offering, to serve in the name of Christ. I have never forgotten the words of one participant at a conference where people had gone on at length about how grace and power abound at ordination, about what the different orders "uphold," "exemplify," or "illuminate" in the church. "Lay people often feel inferior," she said,

> because they do not receive that grace which the clergy receive at their ordination.... Does it not need to be stressed that grace abounds at baptism, at the eucharist, and throughout one's life? Not being ordained does not mean that strength, power, energizing, enabling, will not be available. Sometimes ordination sermons can be very hurtful to the committed lay person.... I would have liked to have heard more about what *lay people* embody, point up, illumine.[28]

My response would be this: The laity point to the diversity of gifts that constitute the body outside the range of ordered ministry. They embody in word and deed the proclamation of the gospel to the world. They illuminate the ever-changing frontier between church and culture in which the gospel must be continually renewed. The skills and gifts of the laity are for the mutual enrichment of the gathered church, where they are in turn strengthened and equipped to be signs of Christ when they scatter.

---

28   Sally Childs, "Response to Borgeson Talk," in *The Diaconate: A Unique Place in Total Ministry*, unpublished proceedings of a conference sponsored by the National Center for the Diaconate and Associated Parishes Inc. held at the University of Notre Dame, South Bend, Indiana, May 31–June 2, 1979, p. 148.

What makes the baptismal ministry of the laity distinctive is precisely its unordered variety, and the freedom and power and creativity that go with it. Baptismal ministry empowers us all to be salt or leaven — choose your image — to the rest of humankind. Defining what the laity do or who they are *only* in terms of the gathered church is like taking away their saltiness or refusing to mix the yeast with the flour. It leaves no hope that the bread will rise.

The words of dismissal at the end of the eucharist are for the entire assembly, clergy included: "Go forth into the world, rejoicing in the power of the Spirit." No Christian is exempt from the baptismal covenant. We need bishops who not only gather the flock and teach the faithful but who go forth into the world to name evil and speak against it. We need presbyters who not only run parishes and preside at liturgies but who go forth into the world to wash dishes and change diapers. We need deacons who not only proclaim the gospel and assist at the altar but who go forth into the world to resolve conflict and give witness to their faith. Above all, we need laity who understand that their particular calling is to be "in the world," to live out the *scattered* dimension of the church's ministry, and who come together with the whole people of God in order to be equipped and supported in that calling.

Bringing the Light of Christ into Places of Darkness

The Diaconate
in the Anglican Church of Canada

Maylanne Maybee

Introduction

One Friday afternoon, as I walked away from my place of work past the cathedral, I saw a clergywoman, elegantly vested in her cassock, standing on the doorstep of the side entrance. She was shepherding in the last of a wedding party — a flower girl dressed in her finest. On the other side of the pathway, at the foot of the war memorial, an old woman lay sleeping, surrounded by her belongings in plastic bags.

A priest, a flower girl, and a bag lady — all within a stone's throw of the church doors, separated by a distance of no more than thirty feet, yet economically, socially, and spiritually worlds apart. The image struck me as an ironic reversal of the wedding feast parable — a feast to which only friends, relatives, and rich neighbours are invited, and from which the poor, the lame, and the blind are excluded.

Scenes like this don't happen only in big cities. They can be recreated in any community. They are scenes that illustrate the chasm between the Sunday congregation and the Monday AA meeting, between the ACW group in the church basement and the Indigenous people who congregate at the bus depot next door, between regular churchgoers and so many others who are imprisoned in hospitals and institutions by illness, loneliness, and old age.

I have a poster showing the head of Christ, and underneath are the words: "How can you worship a homeless man on Sunday and ignore one on Monday?" How can we hold weddings on Saturday, and exclude the poor and the lame the rest of the week? How can we carry the paschal candle at Easter and ignore the darkness for the rest of the year?

The church should be calling the people of God to these places of darkness in our cities and communities, wherever people are separated from God and community by poverty, injustice, or disease. And I believe the church needs deacons to help do this — messengers who proclaim the good news on Sunday and lead the people of God to live it out on Monday. Mediators who make the connection between the church assembled and the church sent forth. Assistants to bishops and presbyters who are living reminders that Christian leadership is rooted in service, and that the church's resources are to be generously shared with the poor.

The church has been ordaining deacons for centuries, well before the priesthood emerged as the normative order. Both the *Book of Common Prayer* and the *Book of Alternative Services* make specific provisions for an ordained diaconate with the dual mandate of caring for the poor and the sick, and assisting the presider at worship. The eucharistic liturgy has always preserved a distinctive role for deacons. The need for diaconal ministry, dedicated to bridging the chasm between the worshipping church and the church in mission, is more urgent than ever. Yet there has been a deep resistance to the idea of restoring this order and ministry to the church.

In this chapter, I wish to clarify what the diaconate might be in our time, to explore the roadblocks and opportunities for renewing a distinctive diaconate, and to make a case for reclaiming the *diakonia* as a sign and vital instrument of the church's mission of reconciliation, justice, and peace making.

A word about terminology: my assumption is that the diaconate is a distinctive, lifelong order that complements the presbyterate and the episcopate. I prefer to avoid adjectives such as "permanent," "perpetual," and "vocational," as they imply that a temporary, impermanent, and non-vocational diaconate is the norm. Despite protests from priests who cling to the notion of "once a deacon, always a deacon," the sacramental visibility of *diakonia* is lost when a person is ordained to another office. I also favour the recovery of the use of the word "presbyter," which has a less sacerdotal connotation than "priest." As I will explain further on, I believe it is at baptism, rather than ordination, that Christians take on the diaconal and priestly character of Christ. Ordination simply highlights and sacramentalizes these Christic qualities of the ministry of all the baptized.

Towards a new understanding
of the diaconate

For too long, the diaconate has been considered an inferior and transitional office — an apprenticeship for those preparing to be "fully" ordained. At best, it has been understood as a kind of mini-priesthood — a designation for special clerical assistants who support the priest. The movement to restore the historic diaconate challenges us to understand it in terms of its own meaning and integrity.

Jesus came into the world as God's agent and messenger. In doing so, "he did not regard equality with God as something to be grasped, but emptied himself, taking the form of a slave" (Phil. 2:6–7). In his earthly ministry, Jesus proclaimed the message of salvation to the poor; he ate among sinners and outcasts; he performed the act of a slave in washing the feet of his disciples. Jesus' example of *diakonia*, or serving leadership, became an essential mark of the church, which is his instrument of service in the world.

We are reminded in John's epistle that "those who love God must love their brothers and sisters also" (1 John 4:21). This kind of caring service to others is expressed in our baptismal vows as central to the life of the church and for every disciple. Just as we speak of the "priesthood of all believers," we can also speak of the "servanthood of all believers."

In the New Testament, we read that seven Christians, "full of spirit and wisdom," received the laying on of hands to be agents of the apostles and to attend to special needs within the community (Acts 6:1–6). In the early church, deacons were responsible for administering funds that were used to care for the poor and people in crisis. They sought out the sick and those in need, and commended them to the congregation for their care. It is on the basis of these roots and traditions that the diaconate is being revitalized and renewed today.

The ordination service for deacons in the *Book of Alternative Services* describes the diaconate in three distinctive ways:

1. *It is a special ministry of servanthood, directly under the authority of the bishop.* Deacons are accountable as "servants" or agents of the bishop, even though they may carry out their duties in a parish setting, alongside a presbyter. As agents of the bishop, deacons support him or her in overseeing the church's mission and service in the world. (Presbyters work together with their bishop and fellow presbyters, and share in the councils of the church. In parishes, they act as the bishop's deputy.)

2. *It is a ministry of service to all people, particularly the poor, the weak, the sick, and the lonely.* The special charge of the diaconate is to

exemplify service and to attend to people in our communities who are the most vulnerable. (Presbyters are entrusted to care alike for young and old, strong and weak, rich and poor.)

3. *It is a ministry of interpretation to the church of the needs, concerns, and hopes of the world.* The diaconate is a reminder to the church that there are others, often not visible, beyond the gathered community who need care, long for justice, and have hope, gifts, and talents to offer. Deacons are called to explain the experience and aspirations of people and institutions "in the world" in a way that invites the church to respond with prayer, compassion, and effective action. (Presbyters are called to be "a pastor, priest, and teacher" to their flock).

The office of deacon is exercised through participation in word and sacrament. What the deacon *does* is shared by all baptized Christians. But the centrality of service is underlined through the diaconate by locating it within one of the ordained offices. This is to make certain that this central mark of the church's life and mission will not be neglected. Such neglect has happened often in the past, and it might well be that such neglect is related to the decline and misuse of the diaconate.

In *service*, the deacon is especially involved in the mission of the church. We tend to think of the church's ministry in terms of its own membership, and often its membership that shows up on Sundays. We increasingly talk of church membership in terms of "congregations," yet the old-fashioned language of "parishes" refers to the church's neighbourhood, to those outside its doors. In our globalized age, the church's neighbourhood stretches across the globe but always begins at our own doorstep. Deacons stand at the threshold between members of the church's congregation and members of the church's parish — local and global. They call attention to people who are excluded from the church's communal life because of illness, isolation, imprisonment, or injustice. They provide example, leadership, and training for the leaders and members of the local church (diocese or parish) to carry out their mission among those who are excluded. Deacons also take initiative in helping the church address the social problems and concerns of the community. They do this especially through advocacy for the needy, neglected, and oppressed, and through appropriate public and political action.

In *liturgy and sacrament*, deacons attend the presider, proclaim the gospel, assist at the altar, and help to administer communion. It is also appropriate for the deacon to lead or coordinate the intercessions as interpreters of "the needs, concerns, and hopes of the world." Through the dismissal, the deacon sends the church in service to the world. Deacons may also carry the sacrament to the sick and isolated.

In the *ministry of the word*, deacons not only proclaim the gospel but may also participate in teaching and preaching, especially if particularly gifted for this ministry and if licensed to do so by the bishop. It is fitting to schedule deacons to speak to gospel passages that focus on the servant character of Christ or the calling into service of all God's people.

The exercise of the office may vary in its particulars. But the person and activities of every deacon must exemplify the centrality of servanthood in the life and mission of the church. Education in the church regarding the diaconate is essential, especially in settings where a deacon serves.

THE PRESENT STATE OF THE DIACONATE IN CANADA

It is apparent, however, that in most parts of the Anglican Church of Canada, our practical theology and ecclesiology have been quite different from this picture. Canada has inherited a monochromatic English model of ministry delivery — paid professional clergy in parish churches. The experience of the diaconate in Canada is largely influenced by this deeply entrenched pattern of church life.

In the larger urban dioceses of Canada, a climate of resistance or indifference to the restoration of the diaconate has prevailed for many decades. Parishes with full-time paid clergy who have used lay volunteers as chalice bearers, pastoral visitors, and church administrators tend to equate the diaconate with these roles and see it as an unnecessary layer of clericalism. Church professionals who work in diocesan centres or multi-staff parishes are often dubious about the introduction of an ordained office that would potentially duplicate or devalue their role in the church.

In less populated or more far-flung dioceses, where seminary trained clergy are in short supply and budgets are limited, the practice may have been to use lay readers or catechists to supplement the Sunday ministry of presbyters. Their responsibilities would include leading morning prayer, delivering homilies (their own or one prepared for them), sometimes administering pre-consecrated bread and wine, and otherwise filling in where needed. In these instances, the diaconate may be regarded as a non-stipendiary supplement to the work of stipendiary priests, "legitimized" by the authority associated with ordination. Understandably, experiments with the diaconate in these circumstances have tended to be confusing and frustrating.

As well, the ordination of women to the priesthood since 1976 virtually wiped out the tradition of diaconal ministry, which for so long had been sustained, exemplified, and pioneered by deaconesses. While they served with dedication, usually in places where male clergy would not go, many experienced exploitation and neglect, and did not become enthusiastic proponents of the restoration of this order.

In the early 1980s, there was a flurry of interest in the diaconate in Canada, attributable perhaps to the influence of what was happening in the Episcopal Church of the USA, to the rethinking surrounding the question of the ordination of women, and to the work of preparing a new *Book of Alternative Services*. Ecumenical dialogues between Anglicans and other communions, especially with Lutherans, are also contributing to a rediscovery of the meaning and purpose of ordained offices, including the diaconate.

At General Synod in 1986, a resolution authorized a task force to prepare guidelines for the restoration of a distinctive diaconate. The subsequent General Synod of 1989 adopted the proposed guidelines handily. In 1991, the Provincial Synod of Ontario officially lifted a long-standing moratorium against ordaining "permanent" deacons, and accepted a set of guidelines to restore the diaconate, based on the 1989 General Synod report.

Despite its leadership, General Synod has no binding jurisdiction over individual dioceses, who can act or not act as they choose. And establishing a common understanding and practice for selecting, ordaining, and using deacons requires commitment, or at least permissive neutrality, on the part of a diocesan bishop. Some dioceses have acted independently to ordain deacons, sometimes despite, sometimes with the consent of, a majority of clergy or laity. Others have adopted a "wait and see" mode. In the latter part of the 1990s, more and more dioceses have quietly introduced the diaconate, which is now a fact of life in at least one-third of the dioceses of the Anglican Church of Canada, and is gradually taking root in every ecclesiastical province.

In any case, the question of a distinctive diaconate is one that will not go away. As funds and church membership decline, it is becoming increasingly difficult to maintain a model of ministry that relies exclusively on professional stipendiary clergy. As the boundaries between the church and society become more sharply defined, there is greater opportunity to use deacons in partnership with presbyters to mobilize Christians to relate meaningfully to the world around them.

In a 1982 paper entitled "The Diaconate: Servanthood Not Slavery," Dan Meakes, at the time a deacon in the diocese of Cariboo, proposed certain criteria to consider in restoring the diaconate. What is required, he wrote, is a framework that is consistent with our context for ministry, consistent with tradition, and effective in its implications. But can we establish a servanthood within an institution, a community, the church, which historically has been oriented towards self-preservation? The re-establishment of the diaconate challenges the very integrity of the Christian community and its willingness to live out Christ's example of ministry among the poor. Meakes points to the largely middle-class membership of the church, and the church's preference to associate mission with evangelism and church growth rather than caring for the poor.

> There are many practical choices to be made with respect to the diaconate which have vast theological implications. Deacons ordained for the sake of a multitude of convenient reasons will result in slavery. Deacons in the context of renewal of mission and the Total Ministry of the *laos* have the potential of establishing a new relationship between Church and World, or Christian Community and dominant Society.... We will hope that our practical decisions are faithful to the ministry of servanthood expressed by Christ.[29]

Dan's paper was written out of the experience of a frontier church with a variety of communities and needs, and closely associated with the Episcopal Church of the USA. Another paper, written

---

29   Dan Meakes, "The Diaconate: Servanthood Not Slavery." 1982.

the same year by Bruce Pellegrin for the bishop of Ottawa, reflects the context of a large, populated, relatively affluent and urbanized diocese in Ontario. He argues that

> the needs of society demonstrate a subtle but real calling of the church to make present the servanthood-caring of the Christian community and that this can be best effected by persons who know themselves to be specially called and commissioned to that function.[30]

My own position is that the church must decide what it wants to do and develop the leadership to support it. Until recently, the situation has not encouraged Anglicans to engage in diaconal ministry or to consider the diaconate as a vocation. The diocesan, congregational, and parish structures of the church have been designed to support the gathered worshipping life of the Christian community. Capital resources have been used to construct or maintain buildings for worship, Christian education, and congregational fellowship. Resources for education have been dedicated to theological colleges preparing students for parish priesthood. Training and continuing education opportunities have emphasized skills in liturgy, preaching, Christian education, individual pastoral care, and counselling.

As Pellegrin points out,

> the present structures appear to force a candidate for ordination into accepting priesthood or nothing. They are surrounded by models of ministry geared towards the presbyterate, they are faced by institutions who see the

---

30 Bruce Pellegrin, "The Diaconate as Vocation and Ministry": A Paper prepared at the Request of the Bishop of Ottawa for the House of Bishops in Aylmer, Quebec, October 1982; p. 2.

presbyterate as the ultimate goal, they deal with Diocesan structures and Canon law that presuppose presbyteral ordination and stipend.[31]

There has been some support for leadership in ministries of justice and social care. The church has done faithful work in the areas of development and global education, Indigenous justice, chaplaincy to hospitals and prisons, ministry among refugees, people of low income, and other displaced people. In the1960s through to the early 1980s, the Canadian Urban Training Project (CUT) trained scores of clergy and laity alike in skills of analysis, social change, and building partnerships with people of low income. The Centre for Christian Studies has trained women and men from the Anglican and United churches in diaconal and social justice ministries. The ecumenical coalitions have earned a stellar reputation for their work in the areas of human rights and global economic justice.

Yet the systemic bias towards the presbyterate has been consistently reinforced by the economic structure of the church. Whereas many parish ministries and chaplaincies are, or could be, self-supporting, diaconal ministry not only does not contribute financially to the life of the church but actually costs it money. Opportunities to do professional ministry in areas of justice, advocacy, and peace making are generally limited to positions in para-ecclesiastical organizations, which often pay less than parish ministry, are less secure, and usually require higher levels of accountability and justification.

The larger issue is that the church does not uphold this aspect of its ministry as the work of every congregation and the calling of every Christian. Professional priesthood has been the dominant model for ministry, and too often "lay ministry" has been regarded as an extension of priestly functions by volunteers. When I think

---

31 *Ibid. p. 9*

of a renewed diaconate in the church, I'm not talking about another layer of clericalism, but another kind of leadership — one that is not primarily pastoral (that is, corporate or gathered), but directed outwards, supporting the people of God to define and undertake ministry outside the church, continually calling the church to look beyond itself to the world that God loves.

MINISTRY, ORDINATION, AND THE DIACONATE

The restoration of a renewed diaconate as part of the church's ordained leadership calls for greater clarity in our understanding of ministry and ordination. Increasingly, baptismal ministry is seen as the work of the *laos*, the whole people of God, for which all Christians are empowered by baptism. This work includes not only the gathered worshipping life of the church, but also the mission of the church, sent forth and dispersed into the world. We speak of the priesthood of all believers, called by baptism to continue in the tradition of the apostles, to resist evil, and to continually repent and return to the Lord. So too we can speak of the *diakonia* of all believers — called by baptism to proclaim the good news of God in Christ, to seek and serve Christ in all persons, to strive for peace and justice among all people, to respect the dignity of every human being. The servant aspect of *diakonia* in particular involves the caring for the "little ones" (*anawim*) of society without expectation of return.

Sceptics about the diaconate often ask, "Why should we ordain deacons to do what lay people can do already?" This gets at the heart of confusion about ordination. The professionalization of ministry in the hands of the ordained has given lay people the powerful message that there are certain things they "can't" or "aren't allowed" to do. Priesthood is commonly understood as something in the possession of certain individuals through ordination. Our language reinforces this: we say that priests "celebrate the eucharist," that they "marry" couples, "absolve" penitents, or "bless" individuals. What we are really saying is that ordination has conferred on them special powers and privileges that other Christians do not possess.

We need to reclaim an understanding of ordination. Ordination is the church's way of selecting and designating persons to whom certain symbolic and leadership roles have been assigned. If priesthood is properly viewed as a characteristic of the people of God, then it is the gathered *laos* who celebrate the eucharist, it is the couple who do the marrying, it is God-in-community who absolves, blesses, and reconciles. Presbyters are ordained not to do these things instead of other baptized Christians, but to point to Christ the High Priest, who does them in our midst. In the same way, deacons are ordained not to do things instead of other Christians, but to point to Christ the Deacon, who came to serve rather than be served.

As leaders, bishops provide oversight at the diocesan level in matters relating to tradition, catholicism, unity, and ecumenism. At the parish level, presbyters give leadership in matters relating to worship, fellowship, spirituality, and reconciliation. Both bishops and presbyters preside at the eucharist, and help the whole community — parish or diocese — to develop a corporate ("pastoral") life, to show mutual care, to strengthen unity, and to overcome divisions. Liturgically, they express this by gathering the people together, pronouncing absolution, saying the blessing over bread and wine, and presiding at other important events such as baptisms, weddings, and funerals in the lives of individuals and the community.

In the same way, deacons give leadership at both the diocesan and local level to the church's mission and service in the world. Deacons should be chosen for their ability to support people to tell their story as baptized Christians; to invite prayer for and effective response to those who are poor, lonely, sick or dying; to identify personal gifts and community resources and direct them towards opportunities for service. These duties have a logical connection with the liturgical duties of the deacon in the eucharist — proclaiming the gospel, leading the intercession, receiving the gifts, doing table service, dismissing the people, bringing communion to those who are sick, dying, or shut in.

The practice of equating "ordained ministry" with paid professional work in the church has muddied the waters. I find it helpful to distinguish between the ordained *offices* of bishop, presbyter, and deacon, whether paid and professionally trained or not, and multiple other forms of *ministry*, which might be stipendiary or non-stipendiary, volunteer or professional, commissioned or ordained, elected or appointed, lifelong or short term.

A minister, then, is someone who does public ministry and is held accountable for that ministry in the name of the church. Among the church's ministers, bishops, presbyters, and deacons are officers whom the worshipping community has chosen and ordained to relate to them in a sacramental way. There is no reason why accountability for ministry cannot be applied with equal rigour to employees, officers, volunteers, and professionals of the church. At the same time, other baptized Christians may participate informally, according to their gifts and resources, in a diverse range of ministries in the home, workplace, and community, but not necessarily with the same level of accountability as ministers who are paid or ordained or both.

Within an inclusive framework, we are still struggling to become clearer about the levels and distinctions of leadership associated with ordination. I believe that orders are signs to the church of her nature, life, and mission. They do not deprive the people of God of their ministry of priesthood or of diaconal service to others. Rather, they spotlight that ministry, hold it up, and encourage it to happen. I believe that "lay ministry" includes those in orders, that it is both priestly and diaconal, and that it is done by the *laos*, the whole people of God. In the eucharistic liturgy especially — the "life work" of the church — we are reminded, inspired, and encouraged to continue that work in our daily lives.

Practical Applications

The challenge, of course, is to give concrete realization to a vision of the diaconate and diaconal ministry, of diminished clericalism and enhanced ministry undertaken by the whole people of God. It means helping people to unpack and unlearn deeply held assumptions. It means de-roling a generation or two of clergy whose self-understanding is more sacerdotal than presbyteral. It means unlearning the idea that "ministry" is what clergy do in the church, and teaching instead that it's what people do in their lives. And it means leading the church to look beyond itself to the society of change, need, suffering, and hope around it.

My own experience with the diaconate has been in the diocese of Toronto. When the ecclesiastical province of Ontario adopted guidelines for the diaconate, and lifted the moratorium against ordaining people to be deacons who did not intend to become presbyters, the diocese of Toronto struck a task force on the diaconate. The task force met for two years to study different models, and to establish diocesan guidelines and procedures before hiring a coordinator (myself to begin with) to put them into practice. Some features of the guidelines and procedures initially adopted in 1994 are worth noting.

1. *The revival process is one of both an office and a ministry.* Individuals may not be ordained deacons except in communities that are also prepared to commit themselves to participate in diaconal ministry.

2. *The model for discernment does not encourage individuals to "self-select" for ordination.* A call or vocation to a ministry that uses one's God-given talents and gifts in a particular place may not be the same as being called by the church to be ordained. Suitability for ordination to the diaconate requires the ability to set an example and inspire others to practise servant ministry, to interpret and

explain what ministry is, and to take a role in the liturgy confidently, gracefully, and audibly. It also requires that these abilities are perceived by the nominating community, not just felt by an individual. Thus, parishes rather than persons are encouraged to make application, with the full endorsement of the incumbent and advisory board.

3. *There is still much to learn about appropriate methods for discernment and nomination that are fair and supportive to individuals and communities alike.* Some excellent resources are available to equip congregations with the education and discernment that they will need to nominate and work with a candidate for the diaconate. Our experience is that congregations are often reluctant to take on the responsibility for nominating candidates, especially if one or two are hovering eagerly in the wings. We have also learned that if competition develops among prospective candidates in a given community, the process should be halted immediately.

4. *Deacons are expected to serve, at least initially, in the communities that nominate them.* They are officers of the wider church, but not in isolation from the communities that authorize them to serve. In cases where a deacon moves, it will be the decision of the bishop and the receiving community whether that person will be licensed to an active diaconate.

5. *"Formation" and "training" are distinct but related components in preparing and supporting individuals for diaconal ministry.* All candidates will undergo a similar formation process to help them to understand their identity as deacons, their liturgical role, their relationships with bishops, presbyters, other deacons, and baptized Christians, and also with families, work colleagues, and the unbaptized. The assumption is that deacons already have some kind of professional identity and training (as teachers, nurses, firefighters, chaplains, etc.).

6. *Additional training will vary with each candidate, depending on their experience and the requirements of their community.* In some cases, candidates will need to develop skills that will help them to be interpreters — for example, group leadership, social analysis, community organizing, conflict resolution, adult education, public speaking. Other skills might include supervision, singing, planning, and volunteer management. These are decided in consultation with an assigned mentor and the sponsoring community.

7. *Deacons are expected to be mature in their knowledge and practice of the faith, but not to have above average expertise in disciplines such as scripture, doctrine, church history, or spirituality.* If they want to increase their confidence or knowledge in any of these areas, they are encouraged to do so for their personal growth and faith development. The assumption is that deacons are primarily "interpreters of the world" rather than teachers of faith and doctrine.

8. *Deacons will not normally be paid by the church, though there are some instances where this will be desirable.* In order to model a new kind of leadership in the church that does not assume clerical privilege, they are encouraged not to use clerical titles and dress. They will not qualify for benefits extended to clergy (housing, pension, tax breaks, etc.) except if they are employees of the church. One consideration is to give deacons voice and no vote at synod, where they interpret "the needs, hopes, and concerns of the world" as part of the synod agenda.

9. *The standard for time given directly to the church is eight hours a week.* The diocese and parishes are expected to budget for reasonable compensation or honoraria for travel, continuing education and related costs, and to clarify arrangements at the time of appointment.

Toronto introduced the ministry of deacons by preselecting a few parishes to pilot the process of choosing and using deacons. The emphasis was on shaping a process on a small scale, rather than laying on a detailed program. Members of the diocesan synod were fully informed of the work of the task force, but the bishops were the ones who gave the approval to proceed. Parish clergy were invited to events where they could learn about the diaconate, express concerns, and make suggestions. After some evaluation, it is expected that adjustments will be made and a more programmatic structure will emerge. The hope is that pilot parishes will show by example the difference that can be made to the life and mission of the church through having deacons in their midst.

We live in a time when churches are weakening, at least in the Western world. They no longer have the membership, the money, the prestige, or the credibility that sustained them in the past. In pastoral situations, when someone is suffering from loneliness or self-pity, we often recommend that he or she undertake volunteer work, and start offering gifts of time, attention, and care to others who are hurting or in need. It's a simple cure, and one that we need to prescribe to ourselves — our parishes and dioceses. I believe that restoring the diaconate as a symbolic and practical ministry of servant leadership is one way of moving boldly forward, of reclaiming the spirit of repentance, justice, and care to which John the Baptist first called his disciples by the Jordan River, and which led them to recognize and receive the greater spirit of compassion and transformation manifested by Christ the Deacon.

PRIESTLY
MINISTRY
Invoking the Truth about God to
Evoke the Truth about Human Lives

Michael Thompson

With a group of Christians from across Europe, I was meeting with members of a Christian youth group in Weimar, East Germany. It was Maundy Thursday, and the next day, with over a hundred Christian young people, I would read one of the scripture lessons in a re-enactment of the way of the cross at Buchenwald, where we would seek for Christ among the bones and ashes of a death camp. In this gathering, in the lounge of a local church, people drifted into twos and threes after the formal presentations, and I found myself talking, in a mix of halting German (me) and more competent English (her), with a young woman of nineteen. In a few days, I would be celebrating Easter with a community of Orthodox, Lutheran, Anglican, and Evangelical Christian young people at a Lutheran conference centre at Erfurt. But tonight I was trying to understand the events of 1982. I had heard of the "Free German Youth," the East German version of the Young Communists, and I asked my companion about it. "Oh," she said, "by the time they're twelve years old, everyone knows it's a fraud." "What do they do with that knowledge?" I asked. "Some turn to alcohol, and some to drugs. Some become involved in sports, and some in vandalism. Some stay involved with Free German Youth, because it is the way to succeed in this society. Some become depressed or antisocial, and some come to the church." "And you," I enquired, "why have you come to the church?" Her response will haunt me forever. "Because here I can say what I am thinking. Here I can speak the truth about my life."

In 1984, the bishop of Edmonton ordained me to priestly ministry. In the intervening seventeen years, I have shared the privilege of exercising that ministry in partnership with fellow presbyters and with those who gather for worship, learning, and service in a number of churches. With a hiatus of almost four years as a university bureaucrat, through marriage and the birth and development of three children, through (I counted them just yesterday when our youngest asked me) ten homes, I continue to be both intrigued and inspired by the witness of a nineteen-year-old whose name I have forgotten. It is to her words that I turn when I need to ground priestly ministry in the reality of God and world.

The church's ministry to that young woman was a priestly ministry. Invoking the truth of God, it evoked for her the presence of God, and drew out of her life its own truth. Invoking the truth of God to evoke the truth of human lives: embodying the truth of God to empower persons to embody the truth in their own lives — these are marks of priestly ministry as the work of the church.

The ordination rite of the Anglican Church makes these marks clear. The setting that is assumed for ordained priesthood is a community of Christians, in the midst of which the priest is called to function in service to its members. "You are to love and serve the people among whom you work," says the bishop, who then continues, "In all that you do, you are to nurture Christ's people from the riches of his grace, and strengthen them to glorify God." Especially when these admonitions are juxtaposed with the baptismal covenant, with its emphasis on ministry in daily life, it becomes clear that the "end user" of priestly ministry is the world. It is the world that is enriched when Christians are nourished by grace to glorify God. It is the world that is enriched when Christians are empowered to live by the baptismal covenant. It is the world that is enriched when Christian people embody the truth of God in the truth of their own lives.

THE PRESENT CRISIS OF PRIESTLY MINISTRY

When the Berlin Wall fell, I sat in the Senior Common Room of Trinity College in Toronto, and mused with a colleague about the reports that had begun to emerge about the new freedom of the East German people. In that day's papers were reports of people flocking to Frankfurt to buy toaster ovens and stereo equipment. As global consumerism threatens to engulf the human spirit with endless variations on stuff, status, and power, the priestly authority of the church to invoke the truth of God and evoke the truth of human lives is a critical dimension in securing a humane future.

It is ironic that our sense of priestly ministry in community is most needed at exactly the same time as we struggle for clarity and confidence about it. Priesthood is under considerable stress, in the lives of those ordained to priestly ministry, and in the communities they are called to serve. Clarity about the essential tasks of priestly ministry has given way to confusion. Any sense of religious obligation has all but disappeared, and per capita participation in Christian congregations is shrinking. The God to whom priestly ministry points, and the institutional forms by which we point, have become less real and compelling to our contemporaries. The growing number who say, "I'm spiritual but not religious" are, in effect, also saying, "Ordained priesthood and the institution in which it is found have no meaning for me." It is no exaggeration to speak of a crisis in priesthood. It is a crisis at once both deeply personal and unrelentingly social. That is to say, it is a crisis both of persons in priestly ministry, and of the structures, assumptions, worldviews, and contexts by which priesthood is what it is.

The "structural" crisis of priesthood emerges out of a complex and often opaque history. The appearance of presbyters in the early church is, in large part, a strategic initiative of delegation, by which the bishop remains connected to the growing number of local congregations by appointing a presbyter to serve on his behalf. This act of delegation is recalled today in the rites provided for induction of a priest into a new ministry setting.

In addition to the act of delegation by the bishop, both the ordinals and the rites of induction (or "Celebration of a New Ministry") retain vestiges of the early practice of the church, by which presbyters were identified and raised up by local communities. Rather than being ordained to a profession or a guild, presbyters were ordained to local ministry. The Council of Chalcedon enshrined this practice in principle, forbidding what it called "absolute ordinations."

The emerging vision of priesthood in the early church pointed to a ministry that was both rooted in the local community (which identified the priest from among its members) and accountable to a wider "catholic" dimension of the body of Christ through the bishop (who lays on hands and invokes the Holy Spirit).

While both of these dimensions are nominally affirmed in the ordination and induction rites of our church, they do not weigh heavily in practice. What has emerged as the dominant expression of ordained priesthood in the Anglican Church of Canada is a guild of professionals who compete with one another to manage a local franchise. Theological education for ordained priesthood takes place, for the most part, in urban centres that are detached from local churches. The process by which priests are appointed to local leadership, while nominally in the authority of the bishop, is in fact driven by "comparison shopping." Clergy compete with one another for the "best" jobs, and the real decision is taken by a group that the congregation appoints, often in response to a narrow mandate focused on the survival of the local church or the maintenance of its current arrangements. Successful franchise management is overtly rewarded by the opportunity for advancement. Priesthood, which at one time resided in community and was embodied in a member of that community, is now, for all practical purposes, the property of the ordained person. Collegiality and a commitment to the catholic nature of the church, while nominally valued, are for the most part undervalued and rewarded faintly, if at all. The priest as "lone ranger" dominates the practice of ministry, even if the theory, as articulated in rites of ordination and induction, espouses something else.

This model of priesthood emerged as a strategy for mission in the period that Loren Mead, in *The Once and Future Church*, identifies as Christendom.[32] Beginning with Constantine's embrace of Christianity as an imperial strategy, and ending in the middle of the twentieth century, churches, especially "mainline" churches such as the Anglican Church, functioned as partners in imperial expansion. The local church related to mission by providing a stable base from which resources could flow to a distant mission field. The qualities valued in local churches were stability, predictability, and a willingness and ability to function as a resource depot through which resources for distant mission could flow. At the edge of the empire, those resources served the expansion not simply of Christian witness but of the economic, political, and cultural assumptions in which that witness was entangled.

Ordained priesthood has taken its cues from the mission of the church. A hundred or even fifty years ago, that mission called for stability at the centre — in the congregations of the "developed" world — and the ability and willingness of those congregations to use their resources for mission work somewhere else. Leaders who could sustain such stability and foster such willingness were highly

---

32   Loren B. Mead, *The Once and Future Church: Reinventing the Congregation for the New Mission Frontier* (Washington, DC: Alban Institute, 1991).

valued. In the formerly "mainline" churches, local mission had been completed, society was defined as Christian, and priestly ministry entailed a stable and predictable round of worship, formation, and pastoral care. People were trained in Sunday school and prepared for life passages at adolescence (confirmation), early adulthood (marriage), childbirth (baptism), and death. Ordained priests managed communities and were, for the most part, providers of the church's ministry. In return, lay people supported the stipend for the priests and other local costs, and contributed either directly or indirectly (through allotments) to the distant missions sponsored by the church.

THE CRISIS IN PRIESTHOOD IS A CRISIS ROOTED IN THE CHURCH'S SELF-UNDERSTANDING IN MISSION

Loren Mead and others help us to understand and acknowledge our own dawning awareness that much has changed. Local congregations are no longer stable, and the mission that they serve is no longer distant. Mission now is local, and in many ways counter-cultural. The church is no longer among the forces that influence the direction of society. A minority of children receives any deliberate Christian formation. A minority of adolescents — even those whose families are on parish lists — seeks confirmation. It is no wonder that there is a crisis in priesthood. The mission that sustained both the church and its ordained leaders has evaporated, and it is not yet clear what will serve in its place. In the meantime, many — perhaps most — ordained priests live and work as if the former model persisted. For priestly ministry to thrive, in communities and in the ordained priests who serve them, the actions of the church must once again align with a coherent sense of mission. The crisis in ordained priesthood is a crisis rooted in the church's self-understanding in mission.

In *Transforming Mission: Paradigm Shifts in Theology of Mission*, David Bosch offers a starting point for that reflection. He invites us to recover a sense of what he calls *missio Dei*, "the mission of God." Mission, says Bosch, is God's mission. And God's mission is directed towards the world's wholeness. Creating and redeeming are what God does for the sake of the world. [33] The biblical story may be read as God's quest for partners who will share in the mission — share with God in creating what has not been before, and in healing and renewing what has been broken.

To be created in God's image does not mean that we "look" like God but that we are called to "act" like God. The kingdom that Jesus proclaims and embodies is, as William Spohn interprets it, "the world according to God."[34] Out of this perspective on the world, Jesus and his followers live their lives. Almost twenty years ago, I met that young woman in East Germany who had encountered the truth of God. Out of that encounter, she had encountered the truth of her own life, and of the society in which she lived. For human beings, made in God's image, the truth we invoke is the kingdom of God, the world according to God, life understood through God's eyes. And for the church in a time of instability and transition, priestly ministry will focus not simply on reproducing the rituals of memory but also on enlivening the encounter by which God-in-mission becomes powerfully present to "persons-in-the-world."

I say "God-in-mission" because there are other gods. There is a god who is fascinated with religion, with the minutiae of religious observances. There is a god who keeps score in a game we can never win. There is a god for every tribe or community that needs to believe in their moral or religious superiority. But these

---

33 David C. Bosch, *Transforming Mission: Paradigm Shifts in Theology of Mission* (Maryknoll: Orbis Books, 1992).

34 William C. Spohn, *Go and Do Likewise: Jesus and Ethics* (New York: Continuum, 1999), p. 102.

are not the living God, the God of Jesus, who sets us free from all those things so that we may serve the world, sharing in God's mission of justice, wholeness, beauty, truth, and love.

And I say "persons-in-the-world" to distinguish that as one choice among many. There are other ways we define ourselves. There are persons-looking-to-escape. There are persons-choosing-not-to-see. There are persons who live in ways that do not take seriously the given-ness of the world, and choose the part of it that most suits them. They make one part of it into the whole, and deny both the beauty and the wounds that make the world what it is.

My encounter with that young woman almost twenty years ago still resonates because somehow, the truth of God had been invoked in her life, and that truth had evoked the truth of her life. She had caught a glimpse of God in mission, and that glimpse had set her free to live truthfully in the world.

A SOLID GROUND FOR PRIESTLY MINISTRY
PARTNERSHIP WITH GOD-IN-MISSION

God's presence to our current crisis as God-in-mission is both effective and encouraging. We are encouraged by the knowledge that God is not paralyzed by a crisis in priesthood, nor by a corresponding uncertainty about the church's self-understanding in mission. God is actively seeking communion with us, and while a crisis in priesthood and ecclesiology no doubt presents a hindrance to God, it does not render God's activity pointless or futile. God is at work in the world, and the world is transformed and renewed by that work.

But it is not simply a matter of encouragement, or of acknowledging God's effectiveness in the face of human crisis and frailty in priesthood and church. God's presence to the world as God-in-mission is a key to a renewal of the church's self-understanding, and to renewed and functional priestly ministries. God as God-in-mission, who seeks a faithful partnership with persons in that mission, invites us to ground a renewed understanding of church and priesthood in this question: What fosters, nurtures, and extends human partnership with God-in-mission?

This is a question by which we can explore both our heritage and our current reality, and bring heritage and the here and now into a conversation that privileges neither while valuing both. The question provides a hermeneutic lens through which to interpret our heritage and our current reality. Like the Rosetta Stone (or the Captain Marvel Decoder Ring of my childhood), the question allows us to link two dimensions that, on the surface, bear little resemblance to one another. Our heritage, full of biblical characters and epic plots, of lore, rituals, traditions, and structures grounded in the apparent stability of a distant past, bears little resemblance to our experience of contemporary living, with its frenzy, its bottom line, and its sitcom attention span. A society impatient with problems that cannot be resolved within the boundaries of an hour-long drama seems unlikely to engage in conversation with a heritage shaped over millennia, returning again and again to the search for what William Spohn calls "a truth we can live by."[35]

The apparent gap between heritage and the here and now begins to narrow, however, when seen through the eyes of God-in-mission. God-in-mission, for Christians, is primarily understood as embodied in Jesus. This Jesus we follow discloses not only the focus of God's mission, which he proclaims as "the kingdom of God," but also what a human life lived "according to God" might look like. "The world according to God" becomes the lens through which we approach reality.[36] To see the world through

---

35 Spohn, p. 16.
36 *Ibid.*

God's eyes is to make a choice, to alter our awareness by admitting something new to it. It turns our attention away from our institutions and structures, and invites us to look at the world. In fact, we become part of God's turning to the world, part of God's search for human partners in caring for it, part of God's strategy for engaging and sustaining those human partners. By turning to the world, and to lives whose truth God seeks to evoke, we begin to break open the airless vault of today's crisis.

What would it look like to begin with persons-in-the-world? What can we know about them, and how can we know it? What values, principles, and convictions do they espouse, and how do they embody them, if at all? In the past decade, significant research in North America, much of it Canadian, has explored such questions. Everything from *Maclean's* magazine's annual poll to the more religiously focused work of Reginald Bibby and Don Posterski has explored the inner landscape of Canadian life. In the United States, an equally significant body of research has emerged. Without exception, those who explore the lives of persons-in-the-world return with the conclusion that there is an untapped spiritual quest present in the lives of most persons, that this quest takes a variety of forms, and that it has grown increasingly distant from organized religious life. Or perhaps organized religion has distanced itself from the spiritual quest.

In the ministry setting in which I work, interviews with those who do not participate in the life of any organized faith community turned up the following themes in the conversation:

1. a search for self-knowledge and an enduring sense of identity;
2. a search for community;
3. a search for rituals for celebration;
4. concern about the values transmitted in society and a sense of responsibility to pass on values, principles, and convictions (tradition) to the next generation;

5. a need to come to terms with life's brokenness and their own personal flaws, frailty, and error;

6. a desire for an overarching narrative or philosophy to hold the various parts of their life together;

7. a conviction that their lives were intended to make some contribution to the world;

8. a yearning to live with passion and conviction;

9. a recognition that society is not structured in ways that support their pursuit of understanding, tradition, service, identity, community, moral honesty, and passionate living.

To this list, generated in a comfortable middle-class context, one might add the search of many others in society for opportunity, equity, and economic and social justice — a search often expressed in the practical and immediate need for adequate housing, employment, social support for the vulnerable, and adequate resources for the support and development of children. It is clear that many — if not most — in our society are engaged in a quest, and that very often there is a discernible relationship between this quest and God-in-mission.

In T.H. White's *The Sword in the Stone*, a very trinitarian (that is to say, communal) God offers each animal the opportunity to request its form and to choose its parts. Arms became wings, mouths became weapons, skin became shields, hands became oars. The human came last, and said, "I think you have made me in the shape I am for reasons best known to Yourselves, and that it would be rude to change." God responds, "As for you, you will be a naked tool all your life; though a user of tools, you will look like an embryo till they bury you, but all others will be embryos before your might; eternally undeveloped, you will always remain *potential* in our image.... We are partly sorry for you, and partly happy, but always proud. Run along then, and do your best." Then God addresses the human one last time: "We were only going to say," said

God shyly, twisting their hands together, "Well, we were just going to say, 'God bless you.'"[37]

This whimsical but compelling image of God's pleasure at the human's choice celebrates both the vulnerability and the power of persons-in-the-world, as well as the blessing God-in-mission confers on those who have the *potential* to share in that mission. White portrays human beings as human "becomings," laden with possibility but limited by their frailty. He offers us an image of God's internal life of communion reaching out to embrace them. As we set out to understand how persons-in-the-world function, and how God-in-mission seeks out and embraces them, these images of vulnerability, potential, and blessing might guide our reflections.

Reflective observation of contemporary persons in today's world is not, however, the only source for our understanding. Scripture is rich with images, stories, insights, characters, and songs that illuminate the lives of those whom God seeks as partners in mission. From Abraham and Sarah to Saul, Barnabas, and Lydia, we encounter a fairly comprehensive cast of human characters. Devious Jacob wrestles with God and becomes limping Israel. Tongue-tied Moses teams up with Aaron the advocate to litigate God's justice in the encounter with Pharoah. Ruth sticks with Naomi and Naomi's God, in that order. An unnamed woman, operating from the far reaches of despair, scrounges one last bit of hope from somewhere and touches the garments of a miracle worker. Another woman, a Syrophoenican, challenges Jesus' tribal formation, a challenge that Jesus calls "faith." Scripture is insightful and articulate, not only about the God that people meet but about the people God meets. It turns out that there is no special race called "Bible people." There is only a community of "persons-in-the-world" who have caught a glimpse of "the world

---

37   T.H. White, *The Sword in the Stone* (New York: Philomel Books, 1993), pp. 239–240.

according to God." There is good conversation to be had between them and our generation. Such conversation will illuminate not only theology but also anthropology, not only the One sought but also those seeking.

PRIESTLY MINISTRY AND THE INSTITUTIONAL CHURCH

It is into these worlds, biblical and contemporary, populated by searchers, that the gift of priesthood spills out of the life of God. Priesthood is God's gift of communion, costly and deliberate. It echoes the self-giving communion that marks the internal life of God as Trinity and becomes God's self-offering in creation, redemption, and renewal. It is not a gift for the clergy or even for the church, but for the world, for persons in that world, for searchers after truth. It is offered to those who seek justice and to those who seek meaning, to those who hunger for forgiveness and to those who yearn for a place of celebration. It is offered to those who seek healing and to those whose gift of healing seeks deep roots in the source of that gift. It is only when we know in our bones that priesthood is God's service to the world that we can begin to speak of any lasting resolution of the crisis in priesthood, any lasting healing of the church's self-understanding in mission.

The archetypal expression of priesthood for Christians is God's self-offering in the death of Jesus. It is a gift of communion given in the face of — and to overcome — the sin (alienation) of the world. It is a costly self-giving affirmation of friendship between God-in-mission and a human world searching for what God offers. It constitutes God's self-giving in, for, and to the world. Its goal is the sort of communion between God and persons-in-the-world that would allow them to re-enlist in a partnership that they have abandoned, to become once more a people "of God." It is a daring and dangerous dream that brings God to the cross. We can be sure that the dream is bigger than any institution. In fact, our experience of the contemporary world, and the witness of the biblical one, might convince us that our anxious hoverings over the institutional survival of the church are more likely to obstruct than to facilitate the realization of this dream of God for the world.

At the same time, it is the institutional dimension of Christianity that provides continuity across time and space, that endows us as an apostolic and catholic church. It is through structure, and in the lives of those who serve and sustain the structural lives of churches, that it is possible to have a meaningful conversation about a crisis in priesthood and in the church's self-understanding. It is not the mere institutional reality of churches that obstructs God's gift of priesthood to the world, but a pervasive idolatry concerning that reality, and the fading into obscurity of our awareness of God-in-mission and of the vulnerability and potential of persons-in-the-world. Renewal of the church necessarily includes renewal of its institutional life.

Because contemporary communities resist the imposition of normative or prescriptive theories and practices, the renewal of the church's institutional life will emerge, not out of a single overarching theoretical framework but out of the experience and experiments of local faith communities. The ministries described in this book bear witness to a variety of such experiments. What binds them together is not a shared commitment to this or that theory, but to responding to God's priestly risk with priestly risks of their own. In *Constructing Local Theologies*, Robert Schreiter argues that the catholicity of the church emerged out of a complex and lengthy conversation among local churches with divergent experiences, practices, and contexts.[38] What may today be experienced as unity at the expense of faithfulness, or even as unity enforced by tacit and overt threats against the status of the local

---

38   Robert Schreiter, *Constructing Local Theologies* (New York: Orbis Books, 1986).

community, was once a gathering of diverse experiences into a common life. Simply by embracing diverse and even divergent experimental practices, we have begun to move past the pseudo-essentials of superficial sameness and into the true source of the church's unity: our common encounter with God-in-mission. In this sense, the experiments we encounter throughout this book are not expressions of a new overarching theory of priesthood but essential elements in an emerging renewal of priesthood in the lives of those ordained to priestly ministry, in the priestly community of church, and in the world God endows with the gifts of God's own priesthood.

We can heal the word "essential" of its polemic misappropriation in the Anglican Church of Canada by attaching it not to what we do or fail to do but to what God has done, is doing, and will do. It is "essential" that we ground our sense of priesthood not in a professional designation for ministry, or even in the church's common life, but in God's priestly ministry towards the world. And it is essential, not merely tolerable, that we explore and participate in that priestly ministry in diverse and even divergent ways, re-establishing a broad and stable conversational foundation for the renewal of the church's institutional life.

The effect of earlier affirmations of the ministry of the laity has contributed to the crisis experienced by those ordained as priests. In its struggle against clericalism, the church flirted with a "zero sum" approach to lay ministry, in effect empowering lay people at the expense of clergy. A significant number of clergy were dispirited and paralyzed by this approach, and the outcome was not a vibrant and life-giving lay participation in the priesthood of God-in-mission. In fact, one could argue that some such initiatives amounted to clergy and laity fighting over the carcass of Christendom in an internal power struggle that was often oblivious both to God and to the world that God addresses in creation, redemption, and renewal. While clericalism carelessly translated the distinct function of those ordained to priestly ministry into a distinct status, attempts to address that distortion by erasing the functional distinction have not fostered healthy and health-giving churches. As one ordained to a priestly ministry, I believe it is possible to function constructively to foster the divine-human partnership as an expression of my ordination, though, like my colleagues, I am quite capable of betraying that possibility in my own confusion or haste.

TOUCHSTONES TO GUIDE OUR PRIESTLY JOURNEY

I will no doubt continue to feel personally the crisis in priesthood as one ordained to a priestly ministry in the church. The church will continue to struggle with a crisis in its self-understanding in mission. The world and persons-in-the-world will continue to struggle and to search for truth to live by. In the midst of such a struggle, I can identify the shape of some of the touchstones that may guide our journey and encourage us in our frailty and our potential:

1. Priesthood in holy orders, in the church, and in the world, is rooted in the priesthood of God-in-mission. It spills out of the communion of the Trinity with the intention of serving through ongoing acts of creation, redemption, and renewal. Its richest and most daunting expression is in God's self-giving in the death of Jesus, and its compelling power is experienced in the presence of the risen Christ in the life of the world.

2. Participation in the mission of God begins with some awareness of God's kingdom, of the world according to God. Priesthood is a ministry of offering God's perspective to persons so that they may encounter the possibility of partnership with God in tending the world.

3. The priesthood God offers to share with us is offered to persons as they are in the world as it is. A core task of the church is interpreting God's self-giving to persons who seek lasting identity; vibrant community; moral honesty; the sharing of values, principles, and convictions from one generation to another; and compelling practices of celebration — the dimensions of a hidden spiritual quest that cries out to be included in our own sense of partnership with God-in-mission.

4. Priesthood is communal, and not simply the property of the ordained. A core task of those ordained to priestly ministries is to foster, reflect, and affirm the priestly character of the churches they serve. In turn, these communities are called to extend themselves into active engagement with those in the world whom God seeks as partners. In preaching, in sacramental ministry, in teaching, in offering and fostering pastoral care, priestly ministry bears witness to a way of seeing the world that is rooted in God's dream for all creation, a dream embodied in Jesus.

5. The healing of the churches' self-understanding in mission will proceed on the basis of diverse and even divergent embodiments of priesthood. Both those who are ordained to priestly ministries and the communities in which they are called to foster and nurture priesthood will be ill-served by misguided attempts to impose sameness as a proxy for unity. Unity creates the conditions for a continuing conversation, not for a sanitized sameness. Over time, perhaps, new common practices and norms may emerge, but over a time longer than the lifetime of anyone now living. We will not in our lives see a time in which the imposition of such norms and practices will be a faithful reflection of God's self-giving in, for, and to the world.

6. Human beings, and the communities in which they gather, are characterized by a complex interplay of frailty and potential. The priesthood that spills out of the interior life of the Trinity will not, and does not, seek to eradicate this reality. It is out of the interplay of frailty and potential that the blessing of communion with God-in-mission is possible.

There are, of course, other touchstones. Perhaps some of those described above will not stand the test of time or scrutiny. What matters finally is not the survival of this or that collection of touchstones, but the active, honest, and disciplined search for such landmarks as may equip churches for partnership with God-in-mission, and with persons in the world in seeking the world's common good.

"Here I can say what I am thinking. Here I can speak the truth about my life."

THE
EPISCOPATE

Michael Ingham

A "bishop" who has set his heart on a position of eminence rather than an opportunity for service should realize that he is no bishop.[39]

AUTHORITY

Authority for ministry in the church originates with baptism. This has been one of the great theological rediscoveries of modern times. The *laos* — the people of God — constitutes the fundamental order of ministry in the church. Every Christian, by virtue of baptism into the death and resurrection of Christ, is called to be a minister of his gospel. It is for this reason that the gifts of the Holy Spirit are given. And for the same reason the church has from earliest times chosen people to exercise particular ministries, rooting the authority for them in Christ himself through the baptismal community.

---

39   St. Augustine, *City of God*, 19:19.

It is necessary to begin here because we need to remind our-selves that ordained ministry is derivative of the *laos,* and not the other way around. This is particularly important in the case of bishops.

Anglicans have tended to elevate bishops to a level of ecclesi-astical nobility. They walk last in liturgical processions, dress in elaborate haberdashery, receive grand titles — no longer "the Rev-erend" but "the Right Reverend" or "the Most Reverend" — and a higher stipend. They are accorded positions of honour in church and society and, unlike most people today, are elected for life and with a high degree of tenure.

There is keen interest in the process that creates them, and almost no process for removing them. They are the object of rib-ald jokes ("as the actress said to the bishop...") and cruel delight when one stumbles or falls ("French Cardinal Found Dead in Paris Brothel"). Collectively and individually, they are held accountable for the growth or decline of the church, despite such obvious ex-aggeration of their effectiveness. In short, the episcopate looks like a desirable thing to have, if a fearful thing to hold. It is the object of both adulation and contempt.

Yet the image of bishops as supreme monarchs and absolute rulers — occasionally fostered by bishops themselves in moments of insecurity — is perpetuated not so much by long tradition as by the modern church itself. We exhibit some of the co-dependent behaviour of a dysfunctional family. We create the very conditions we want to reject. Both ordained and lay alike are complicit in supporting a system that disables talented individuals, inhibits healthy relationships, and frustrates reform.

I will say more about this later, but it is important to know that bishops have not always been regarded thus in Anglicanism. Rich-ard Hooker, arguably the greatest theologian of the English Reformation, had a "low" view of episcopacy:

> Though bishops may justly claim apostolic descent, yet
> the absolute and everlasting continuance of it they cannot

say that any commandment of the Lord doth enjoin; and therefore must acknowledge that the church hath power by universal consent upon urgent cause to take it away, if thereunto she be constrained through the proud, tyrannical, and unreformable dealings of her bishops.[40]

Hooker regarded the episcopate as a good thing but not a necessary thing. In his view, the purpose of bishops is primarily to be bearers of apostolic faith and teaching.

This understanding led the English church, unlike some of its continental counterparts, to retain bishops in the sixteenth century after the break with Rome. But in the seventeenth century, some discoveries were made of early church documents that had been unknown to the Reformers.[41] They included the second-century letters of Ignatius, Hippolytus, Ireneus, and Cyprian. They contained what we might call a "high" view of episcopacy. Thus:

> Let all of you follow the bishop as Jesus Christ did the Father.... Wherever the bishop appears, there let the people be, just as wherever Jesus Christ is, there is the catholic church. Whatever he approves is also pleasing to God.... He who honours the bishop is honoured by God. He who does anything without the bishop's knowledge is serving the devil.[42]

Ignatius established the bishop as the principal celebrant of the eucharist and, therefore, president of the assembly. Hippolytus asserted that episcopé contains the fullness of the other ministries,

---

40 *Laws of Ecclesiastical Polity*, III.

41 See "The Orgins of the Episcopate" by J. Robert Wright, in *On Being A Bishop* (New York: Church Hymnal, Corp., 1993).

42 St. Ignatius, *Letter to Smyrna*, 8.

so that ordination is to be conferred by the bishop alone. Ireneus declared the bishop to be the principal teacher of the apostolic faith, while Cyprian said episcopacy confers leadership of all church councils and secures the unity of the local church with the universal. Thus, by the second century, the episcopate had become the primary order of ministry from which the other orders were deemed to flow.

This position has profoundly influenced Anglicanism from the seventeenth century until today. It is now customary for the bishop to preside at the eucharist when he or she is present. Non-episcopal ordinations are not recognized. A diocese is understood as a regional grouping of churches gathered around a bishop. Both diocesan synods and national synods give the order of bishops separate voting power. Ordinals in the various Prayer Books throughout the Anglican communion emphasize the universal as well as the local character of the church, with the bishop as the link between them.

Anglicanism continues to embrace both "low" and "high" views of episcopacy (as about many things). There is, however, general agreement across the communion on what is expected of a bishop, and this is expressed, for example, in the Canadian *Book of Alternative Services*:

A bishop in God's holy Church is called to be one with the apostles in proclaiming Christ's resurrection and interpreting the Gospel, and to testify to Christ's sovereignty as Lord of lords and King of kings.

You are called to guard the faith, unity, and discipline of the Church; to celebrate and provide for the administration of the sacraments of the new covenant; to ordain priests and deacons; and to join in ordaining bishops; and to be in all things a faithful pastor and wholesome example for the entire flock of Christ *(p. 638)*.

The newly ordained bishop is given a shepherd's staff to symbolize the office as chief pastor of the diocese, and a Bible as a sign of authority as chief steward of God's word and sacraments. Other elements in the rite stress the self-discipline required of a bishop, prescribing habits of regular prayer and study, the ability to listen and to take counsel, qualities of compassion and truthfulness, and a desire to nourish the spiritual lives of the whole people of God.

It is a daunting task indeed, and those who are given it know its weight. Yet the actual living out of these expectations is fraught with difficulty. This is because they both express and reinforce inherent contradictions in episcopacy itself and in the church as a whole.

Episcopacy in practice

I remember a day early in my episcopate when I entered a room full of friends and colleagues, people I had known for twenty years. I was astonished when they all stood up. In the next few weeks, my jokes suddenly became funnier, my casual observations strangely more profound, and great interest was taken in my well-being in a way never shown before.

Even though I had been elected from "inside" the diocese and was personally known, the process of distancing and elevating had begun. It was well meant, a sign of respect given to the office more than to me, but it had the effect of drawing an invisible veil across long-established relationships. It felt alien and disempowering. I began to sense information was being "tailored" to manoeuvre me in particular directions, and was surprised when an episcopal colleague said, "Two things happen when you become a bishop. You never eat a bad meal, and no one ever tells you the truth!"

I was overwhelmed with demands. Every organization within the diocese wanted me to articulate my "vision" for the church. Every priest and deacon wanted time with me to establish a new pastoral relationship. Those clergy my predecessor had refused to license came to assure me of their undying gratitude for my election.

Every lingering parish conflict turned up fresh at my door. Volumes of mail arrived in truckloads. I was asked to make decisions about matters of which I had no understanding, about which I did not know how to get accurate information. There were staff contracts to negotiate, organizational systems to redesign, critical gaps in diocesan policy to cope with, and confirmations.

Confirmations .... I started out joyously down this road, sweeping into filled churches with expectant and slightly apprehensive faces, enjoying the nervousness of the clergy, sensing the last hopes of parents that perhaps the bishop might be able to get through to their youngsters. I was aware, of course, that confirmation is a sacrament in search of a meaning, but I was determined to seize the moment as an evangelistic opportunity, to inspire the congregation, to catch the imagination of the candidates.

Ten months later my preaching had regressed fifteen years. I had exhausted everything there is to say about confirmation in the first six outings, and the next fifty became a listless repetition. Time pressures left me with no spaces to think or prepare. I began arriving at churches in breathless haste, and composing sermons during the introit hymn. Standing in the pulpit or at the chancel step, I would start to speak with my mind a mere half-sentence ahead of my mouth. The thought of doing this until retirement was appalling.

Other contradictions began to emerge too. I was encouraged by clergy and laity alike to be courageous in leadership, to help the church face the difficult challenges ahead, to be an agent of change as well as of tradition, to speak the truth in love. This was enormously supportive, but when I did speak the truth in love, I was met with howls of disapproval, accusations of apostasy, and even more mail.

Kortright Davis remarks, "When the bishop speaks, everybody listens. So the bishop has to be careful to speak with everybody in mind." This is true, but how hard it is. It can easily become a retreat into inoffensive blandness signalling the loss of integrity. For a bishop, guarding the unity of the church and maintaining the integrity of one's own faith convictions is no easy matter, especially in our theologically polarized climate. There is a deep temptation to moderate rather than to lead.

Openness to other points of view and the capacity to respect the deeply held convictions of other people is an essential characteristic. But so is the gift of discernment and submission to the word of God. Episcopal ministry frequently involves painful choices between faith and unity, between resolving conflicts and making unpopular decisions, and it can feel like a cross on which the soul permanently hangs.

There is a price to be paid for these contradictions in terms of spiritual and physical health. But there is an even greater one to be paid by a bishop's family, where the pain of seeing one's spouse deeply hurt and constantly tired is compounded by the inability to do anything about it, and by the necessity of maintaining a positive public appearance all the while.

Bishop Steve Charleston of Alaska recently resigned his see because of the stress of episcopal ministry on his family life. He said this:

> The episcopacy really needs reform.... I believe the majority of the House of Bishops would say the greatest frustration in their ministry is that they don't feel able to live out a spiritual style of leadership. They find themselves constantly enmeshed in the managerial sides of leadership....
>
> The whole system is designed to seduce a man or woman into a feeling of being constantly involved with all the decisions....
>
> Times for reflection, quiet prayer, daydreaming, conversations, storytelling, listening, walking, looking at the earth — all of those things are not prized. So the temptation is to minimize the spiritual and to maximize the managerial.[43]

---

43 Interview in *The Witness* (December 1995).

Charleston's comments illustrate the dysfunctional family system that is sometimes the church. We ordain bishops to be spiritual leaders, for which they are generally well equipped, and then give them responsibilities of corporate management, for which they are quite untrained. We dress them in purple and fine linen, and then complain about aloofness and hierarchy. We expect them to be people of prayer, wisdom, and learning, and then to attend endless meetings and reply to an avalanche of letters. We make them caregivers to the pastors, then give them great power over appointments and careers, setting up patterns of dependency and resentment for many clergy and their families. We encourage them in a ministry of transformation, but reward them only for actions that promote system maintenance and tranquillity.

In this context, the actual practice of episcopal ministry today does not allow for the fulfilment of episcopal vows. It is no secret that many bishops are unhappy with their roles, just as many in the church are unhappy with their bishops. What can possibly be done?

Reshaping episcopal ministry

I want to make some practical suggestions for reshaping episcopal ministry. All of them arise from a theological understanding of the *laos* — the people of God — as the fundamental order of ministry in the church, essentially reversing the tradition from the second century. We need to re-establish the sacrament of baptism as the primary call to ministry of every Christian.

If this is accepted, it follows that the threefold order of bishops, priests, and deacons is intended to serve and sustain the *laos*, not the other way around. Ordination is the setting apart by sacred rites of persons with special gifts and charisms to support the body of Christ and his mission in the world. We should be enabling these persons to exercise their gifts by releasing them to do what they do best. Systematic obstructions need to be removed by better use of the abilities of others.

Reshaping episcopal ministry must mean recovering the primary apostolic purpose of the office as expressed in the ordinal, and shedding whatever is not found there. This can be summarized in four principal functions.

1. *To proclaim and interpret the gospel of Christ to the church and to the world.* The church today has a profound need for gifted teachers and skilled communicators of the word of God. And in fact, there is a remarkable number of them in our midst. Bishops should be elected from among them. Rather than looking for the candidate most able to represent our theological party, or least likely to offend the largest number, we should call into leadership those whose evident faith in Christ communicates itself authentically and commands the deepest recognition, or else those who can call forth faith in others by inspired instruction and persuasion. Bishops should be teachers of the gospel first of all.

This requires a large degree of freedom from administrative and managerial functions. Supervising offices, spearheading programs, hiring staff, sitting on boards and committees, performing bureaucratic tasks, wading through legal work, preparing budgets, being consulted about every decision — unless these tasks are clearly related to the proclamation and interpretation of the gospel, they are not part of a bishop's purpose, and should not be part of a diocese's expectation. Episcopé is not called forth from people with administrative ability but from people with spiritual ability.

In many Canadian dioceses, however, reform is prevented by financial cutbacks and diminishing diocesan staff, particularly in the north. The Canadian church will have to consider drawing together the administrative and financial functions of separate dioceses into single centralized provincial offices under effective lay leadership, and freeing bishops from unnecessary duties. In some dioceses, as national funding has been withdrawn, bishops may have to retain responsibilities as parish incumbents. The model already exists among Indigenous bishops, and it may need to be extended across the church in more imaginative ways. This in itself would require a change in the role and expectations of bishops.

We should feel free to imagine new models of ministry for bishops beyond current diocesan patterns. In the USA and New Zealand, examples exist of non-territorial bishops, primarily for Indigenous people.[44] Canadian Indigenous people rightly look upon these models with interest, but we may soon have to extend them further if dioceses themselves start to dissolve, for example, in the current crisis of litigation.

Also in England, we have the example of a bishop as a commissioned evangelist with a national ministry of teaching and proclamation. In the USA, a bishop heads up the national program of training for new bishops, and there are several examples of episcopal teams working together in different configurations, as we have also in Canada. There is no reason to restrict the ministry of a bishop to a diocese, any more than to limit a priest's minstry to a parish. Some creative imagination here could make up for the lack of resources. Bishops themselves will have to relax their hold on jurisdiction to allow collegial models to develop.

2. To guard the faith, unity, and discipline of the church. This sounds like an inherently conserving role — the brakes rather than the accelerator. Certainly, in our dysfunctionality we interpret it as such, and discourage bishops from forays into new theological territory or non-traditional approaches to ministry. The effect can be deadly on creative minds. It threatens to reduce the episcopal

---

44   In England and Wales, a similar model provides "visiting bishops" for people disaffected over the ordination of women, but we should treat this as an aberration. Diocese are not political entities of those who agree on certain issues, but ecclesial entities of those who belong to Christ through baptism, and who are in communion with their bishop.

bench to slumbering elders in the grip of terminal caution. But there is nothing about guarding the faith that necessarily requires an overwhelming prudence. No ministry grounded in Jesus Christ could be authentically afraid of risk and the crossing of boundaries.

Maintaining the unity of the church today requires acts of courage and risk taking. In this rapidly changing spiritual environment, old approaches won't do. Genuine faithfulness requires openness to new knowledge, willingness to re-examine accepted orthodoxies in the light of compelling truths in other disciplines such as the arts, sciences, philosophy, and other religions. Guardianship need not mean simply "holding the traditional line." It should also mean preventing spiritual decay and intellectual atrophy. It should mean tossing the occasional hand grenade into the closed rooms of dogmatism that so often passes for Christian education.

Christian orthodoxy, properly understood, has always been open to contemporary intellectual thought, and has sought to use it as a vehicle for the gospel. But there is a massive intellectual fraud being perpetrated on the church today by those who claim orthodoxy to be co-terminous with the repression of theological creativity. The alacrity with which any bishop who utters a speculative idea gets pounced upon is actually depriving the church of the bold leadership it needs.

There is certainly no place for theological recklessness within the episcopate. Rather, a corollary of guardianship is that the church should be equipped to engage the modern world in debate on its own terms for the sake of salvation. The Anglican tradition has been well served by scholarly bishops with the ability to bring Christianity into contact with contemporary thought, and vice versa. Some have been iconoclasts, some rogues, but most have advanced the mission of Christ by making faith accessible to those for whom traditional language and belief are no longer credible or salvific. The church needs to encourage adventuresome bishops as well as conservative ones.

3. *To provide for the administration of the sacraments of the new covenant.* Bishops are to ensure sacramental ministry is everywhere provided for so that the church may be fed and loved. This means the bishop must continue to have authority to ordain and to license. But it also suggests the essential skill of delegation.

One of the duties that ought to be delegated is confirmation. In the Orthodox tradition, confirmation is administered by priests. This is a practice to which we should move, or rather return, for in the Western church confirmation was reserved to bishops only after the sacrament of Christian initiation was divided in two — into what we now call baptism and confirmation. Confirmation by priests would both restore the original unity of Christian initiation and free the bishop to exercise a more apostolic ministry.

In my own diocese, I no longer do parish confirmations (they are held in the cathedral during Easter). This enables me on Sundays to visit churches, to celebrate eucharist, to teach the gospel, to visit clergy families, and to discuss matters affecting the well-being of the parish. It means I am present at normal parish celebrations, and can spend time with people afterwards instead of cutting cakes, posing for photographs, and handing out certificates. It also means I have to preach my way through the eucharistic lectionary without being perpetually tied to the subject of Christian initiation.

Other duties can be delegated too. Most bishops spend inordinate amounts of time in career counselling and personnel redeployment. Parish search committees consume hours of travel and consultation time. Undoubtedly, these can be opportunities for good pastoral contact, and can build a spirit of trust and confidence in the diocese and parish. But few bishops are trained in the increasingly complex field of personnel management and development. No major employer in Canada today expects its chief executive officer to handle the personnel department. Every diocese needs to examine its practice of human resources appointment and development, and where possible, release the bishop from direct responsibility.

4. *To be a faithful pastor and wholesome example for the entire flock of Christ.* As well as the usual things this implies — the striving towards exemplary personal conduct that is the vocation of every baptized Christian, yet without the sin of false moralism or the pride of perfectionism — there are some quite specific things it would be helpful for bishops to model.

One is a healthy attitude towards work. The church resembles a dysfunctional family partly because it rewards and reinforces destructive patterns of work. How often do we praise the faithful pastor who spends all night by a hospital bed, or the parish secretary who doesn't mind being phoned at home? How often do we criticize the priest who has an answering machine in the rectory or doesn't come to every meeting? There is no other profession in Canada where such expectations would be tolerated. Clergy and laity who respond to these expectations, desiring a reputation for diligence and faithfulness, are actually creating the conditions for burnout and depression. They risk not only their own health but that of their families, who have no choice but to play this obsessive compulsive game to their own destruction.

Bishops have heavier work pressures than almost anyone in the church, so one of the most helpful forms of leadership would be for them to renounce compulsive work habits and become wholesome examples of balanced healthy lifestyles. This is not compatible with eighty-hour work weeks or huge amounts of time away from home. A more healthy model would be in the forty-five to fifty-five hour a week range, and this should be a standard condition for all clergy.

Personal health necessitates the sharing of ministry. Collegial models of leadership, rather than lone ranger styles, need to be praised and rewarded. Church members should reinforce health by criticizing bishops and clergy who spend too much time at work, and praising those who are not always available because of clearly set boundaries. Bishops must give support to clergy challenged by unrealistic parish expectations, but should start by making public their own family commitments and needs for personal renewal.

Being a healthy model means abandoning obsessive work addictions. And if the diocese or parish starts to break down and fall apart because of it, so much the better. The road to health in the church may have to begin with the collapse of the present order. People will not take responsibility for themselves while leaders continually take responsibility for them.

Another aspect of episcopal modelling has to do with accountability. Because the ministry of bishops arises out of the *laos*, it must continually be accountable to it. People of the church legitimately require good stewardship of what they entrust to their bishop. This should take the form of regular annual performance appraisals.

In my own diocese I have asked for this, and the diocesan council has set up a process for my annual review. It is not a hostile or threatening process but a helpful one. Properly done, as mine is, it assists me to focus on areas of my strengths and weaknesses, so that I may receive support for the one and direction for the other.

All clergy and lay workers should be evaluated regularly in a pastoral and supportive way. One of the reasons many church employees fear and resist evaluation is that it is often poorly done, and done only when there is a conflict. Then it can be used as a weapon. Evaluation ought to be an instrument of growth and improvement. This is one of many areas where we can learn from industry how to manage personnel issues more professionally and carefully.

The church ought also to look seriously at setting terms for bishops, as for all clergy. The diocese of Kootenay has done this, establishing a ten-year term for the diocesan bishop. The stress of episcopal ministry is such that this should be seen as a preservative measure to free the bishop to move on to other ministry. It also frees the diocese to seek fresh leadership or to renew its relationship with the present incumbent.

Finally, we need to look for ways to diminish the distance that separates bishops from their flock. One would be for bishops to stop what Bishop Richard Holloway at the 1994 Winnipeg Symposium on Ministry called "power dressing." Expensive haberdashery is intrinsically distancing. Why do bishops need to dress in purple? Roman and Orthodox bishops don't, except on liturgical occasions. For ordinary dress, they retain the black stock of the priesthood. Perhaps this is an Anglican distinctive we might rethink. It is a small sign, but then we live by signs.

I remember going out to a small country church one hot summer day, and halfway through the service, when the heat was unbearable, I took off all my liturgical gear, and stood there as an ordinary human being. An audible sigh of relief went through the church! Some sort of barrier had come down.

IN A WORD...

Barriers of all sorts must come down. The reshaping of episcopal ministry requires a restoring of the apostolic nature of the office and the abandoning of historical accretions that have attached themselves to the role, to the detriment of the incumbents and the church. It should begin with a rethinking by bishops of the jobs they have accepted. It will have to be supported by clergy and laity, who must stop expecting bishops to be more than the human beings they are. Such healthy rebellion could help put an end to the dysfunction of our present system, and encourage the liberation of the *laos* to exercise the ministry they have been given in baptism.

BIOGRAPHICAL SKETCHES

David Ashdown was baptized 24 August 1952, and grew up in Saskatchewan, where he attended a one-room country school and received his early Christian education through Sunday school by post and the Sunday school vans. He received his BA from the University of Saskatchewan, then attended the College of Emmanuel and St. Chad, graduating with a BTh and MDiv In 1978, he was ordained. He served in several rural parishes in the diocese of Qu'Appelle, and for two years was a consultant in rural ministry. In 1992, he became executive archdeacon of Athabasca diocese and, in 1999, moved to Keewatin diocese, where he became archdeacon and then bishop.

A former prolocutor of the ecclesiastical province of Rupert's Land, he has served on several national and provincial committees. He has been keenly interested in Indigenous issues, and healing and reconciliation work, for many years. Since 1998 he has been an instructor at TAIP (Train an Indigenous Priest). He is the author of Christian Now, an adult baptismal education program. He lives in Kenora with his wife, Penny. They have three grown children.

Michael Batten was educated at the University of Victoria (MA, 1988) and Vancouver School of Theology (MDiv, 1992), and received practical training in ordained ministry at St. James', Vancouver, and at St. Saviour's Church, Barkerville, in the diocese of Cariboo. He spent seven years in Cariboo (where he spent much of his time driving fire trucks, thus fulfilling a boyhood ambition), serving both rural and urban parishes, including a shared Anglican-United pastoral charge in the beautiful Robson Valley. In 1999, he was called back to St. James' to inaugurate the new chaplaincy at St. James Community Service Society.

Pat Connolly and Sue Garvey
Susan Garvey is the director of Cornerstone/Le Pilier. Cornerstone has three residential facilities for women who have been homeless: The Women's Shelter (the only emergency shelter for homeless women in Ottawa), 515 MacLaren (permanent housing for twenty women), and McPhail House (permanent housing for six women). Sue has a Master's degree in Social Work.

Pat Connolly is the director of The Well/La Source, a day program for women at risk and their children. The Well offers personal, practical, and spiritual support and a sense of community for those who visit each day. Pat has a DWS from Algonquin, a BA in law from Carleton, and is working towards her Master's degree in Theological Studies, with a particular interest in Restorative Justice.

Both Sue and Pat have worked in church based and secular agencies serving low-income women, men, and children in Ottawa for over twenty-five years. Committed Christians, they are dedicated to the social justice model of offering empowering services for people in need, and to working for change in the systems that perpetuate poverty and homelessness.

Robin Duffield was a person of many talents. A part of the leadership team in her parish, she helped to produce the newsletter. After high school graduation, Robin undertook a variety of secretarial positions, both in Regina and locally. Her volunteer activities included the Philharmonic Chorus and the executive of the Regina

Symphony Women's Auxiliary. A member of local Eastern Star and the Legion Auxiliary, she assisted in the publication of a history book. Latterly, as Semans Librarian, she worked diligently to encourage all to enjoy the library. She studied several university courses, and was completing a course on prairie horticulture when she became ill and died on 23 December 2000, after a hard-fought battle with cancer.

David Fletcher is the rector of the Parish of Lantz, near Halifax, Nova Scotia, and was appointed Program Coordinator of the Non-Stependiary Ordained Ministry Program in 1993. The Parish of Lantz makes a gift of 20 per cent of his time to this diocesan ministry. He is presently pursuing advanced studies in congregational development at the Seabury Institute, Evanston, Illinois, and was recently a candidate for bishop in the diocese of Nevada, where most of the ordained are non-stipendiary.

Granvyl G. Hulse, Jr. served with the CIA for twenty-seven years, retiring to Colebrook in 1975. He was ordained in 1987, and served as the fourteenth Vicar of St. Stephen's, Colebrook, until 1998 when he was re-assigned to the Border Parish. He is a past commander of the American Legion Post, a past master of the local Masonic lodge, and for many years has been a grand chaplain of the Grand Lodge of New Hampshire. He is the author of *Modern Lebanese Coinage*, *The Coinage of Modern Ethiopia*, *Evening Star Lodge #37*, *The History of St. Stephen's Episcopal Church, Colebrook*, and *Let's Eat Out*, a history of the restaurants of Colebrook. He has had numerous articles published relating to numismatics and Freemasonry, and was the founding editor of a genealogical quarterly relating to the Hulse families in America. His wife of forty-three years, Helen (Kay) Hulse, passed away in 1996. He has four children, Martha, James, Edwin, and Heather; and ten grandchildren.

Peter Flynn, born during the depression years and raised as a cradle Anglican, studied at Royal Roads and Royal Military College from 1954 to 1957. In 1961, at a retreat Holy at St. John's College, he experienced a "small c" charismatic renewal. He was ordained deacon in 1964 and priest in 1965. In 1967, he was appointed chaplain at St. John's College and the University of Manitoba, Winnipeg, where he served until 1972. In Edmonton, he studied counselling psychology, returning to Winnipeg to become priest associate at River North Anglican Parishes in 1976. From 1981 to 1984, he also served as provincial secretary to the Advisory Committee on Postulants for Ordination (ACPO).

An enduring interest in ecumenical cooperation came to fruition in 1986, when he was appointed rector of St. Matthew's, Winnipeg, a United/Anglican shared ministry. He has also maintained an enduring interest in and commitment to the church's ministry of peace and justice. During a sabbatical leave in 1995, he studied different models of inner city ministry in Great Britain, returning in 1998 to revisit certain sites. In 1991, he helped to organize *Ancient Roots, New Routes*, a national conference to celebrate the origins and future of justice ministry in the Anglican Church. He is also a member of the steering committee of *Magnificat*, a national network of Anglicans concerned with peace and justice.

On 31 December 2001, Peter will retire from St. Mathhew's, after which he expects "to find surprising new opportunities to serve."

Michael Ingham is the author of *Mansions of the Spirit: The Gospel in a Multi-Faith World* and *Rites for a New Age, Understanding the Book of Alternative Services*. After graduating in theology from the University of Edinburgh, he studied at the Hebrew University in Jerusalem and the Center for the Study of World Religions at Harvard. He was ordained in 1974, has served in parish ministry, and was principal secretary to the Primate of the Anglican Church of Canada. He is now the bishop of New Westminster, and lives in Vancouver, British Columbia, with his wife and children.

Kimiko Karpoff has turned her communications background towards activism and advocacy on affordable housing and other social justice issues at the community level, including two years with New Westminster Reachout. She is currently an advocate with the Lower Mainland Network for Affordable Housing. She has continued to write the "Reaching Out" column in the *Royal City Record* and contributes occasionally to the Anglican newspaper, *Topic*, the *Vancouver Sun*, *SPARC News*, a publication of the Social Planning and Research Council of BC, *BC Christian News*, and *Adbusters* magazine. At St. Barnabas, she has found a welcoming community that nurtures her faith and her belief in social justice.

Mark Kinghan has been ordained since 1989 and has served as the incumbent of St. John's Anglican Church, Weston, for nine years. In cooperation with the Reverends Betty Jordan and Mary Pataki, Mark is currently developing a consultation team, The Community Explorers, who will help churches hold up a mirror to their community and reflect on their ministry of presence. For Mark, it is a privilege and a humbling experience to share the neighbourhood ministries, both at the parish of St. John and ecumenically through the cooperative efforts of the Weston area churches.

Roslyn Macgregor was born and educated in Montreal. In 1967, she became a Sister of St. Margaret in Boston. Two of the following nine years were lived in Haiti. In 1975, she suffered a breakdown (in retrospect, breakthrough). Upon her return to Montreal in 1983, she completed a BA in Child Studies/Education, and then earned a diploma in Theological, Religious, and Ethical Studies at Concordia University. In 1990, she finished an MA in Etudes Pastorales at l'Université de Montréal, followed by the In-Ministry year at Montreal Diocesan Theological College, before ordination as deacon in 1991 and as priest in 1992. After two years as a curate and a brief period of being unemployed, she landed on her feet in two half-time ministries: a traditional parish and Mile End

Community Mission. Her experiences of hospitalization, therapy, and of Haiti are the events that most dramatically affected her understanding of herself, humanity, and the world, and prepared her for ministry "on the edge."

John A. (Ian) MacKenzie, is the recently retired Archdeacon of Caledonia (1982–2000) and former director of the Native Ministries Program at the Vancouver School of Theology (1989–99). He is an adopted Haida and an adopted Nisga'a, and served in two First Nations congregations in order to facilitate the development of local lay and ordained ministries. He was an appointed member of the Nisga'a Tribal Council from 1979 through to the election of the first Nisga'a government under the new treaty in November 2000. He has been active in implementing new forms of ministry in the diocese of Caledonia, including the development of testing, selecting, and training processes for men and women identified by their own congregations as candidates for ordained ministries. He was the director of the Caledonia Ministry Development Program (1982–96), and helped establish the Theological Education by Extension Centre in Terrace, BC. Ian was a key person in the creation of the Native Ministries Consortium and the first accredited extension Master of Divinity program at the Vancouver School of Theology.

Maylanne Maybee was raised in a diplomatic family and nurtured in the Anglican tradition. Before turning eighteen, she had lived in Australia, the US, and Lebanon, as well as Ottawa, Canada, and had learned to speak French fluently. "I travelled with family and friends in Europe and the Middle East, where I visited and worshipped in Anglican, Roman Catholic, and Orthodox churches. The sight of Palestinian refugee camps in the outskirts of Beirut during the 1960s made me sensitive to the condition of uprooted and displaced people. At the same time, the images and messages of scripture kindled a compassion for the poor and a zeal for justice."

After graduating in Modern Languages from the University of Toronto in 1971, she studied education and theology in Oxford, England. Upon her return to Canada, she became director of Christian education in a Toronto parish, and taught religious education in a private girls' school. In 1978, she became a deacon, and continued to raise a family, teach, and work towards a Master of Divinity at Trinity College, Toronto. She was encouraged to be ordained, but in 1981, following a conference in the US about the diaconate, she knew she "wanted to remain a deacon, as it seemed to emphasize ministry with people at the edges of society and systems, where I felt truly called to be."

She became involved in housing, health, and literacy projects for people of low income in Toronto's Parkdale neighbourhood, and in 1986, she was hired to work with the Urban Core Support Network, a church-based network that linked organizations and people across Canada who were doing grassroots anti-poverty work. From 1992 to 1996, she helped to start up a national foundation to support community non-profit housing, and worked for the diocese of Toronto to start up a program for deacons. In 1996, she was the coordinator for Mission and Justice Education at the national office of the Anglican Church of Canada. Currently she is the coordinator for Justice Education and Networks.

"Working for social transformation, being with those at the edges, and 'doing' theology, liturgy, and education, have been my abiding passions. It has been a privilege and a challenge to collect and edit the stories of others who are passionate about their ministry, and willing to take risks to help make new things happen."

Michelle Moore and a few other parishioners decided, with the blessing of Bishop Eric Bays, to continue church services when their parish could no longer afford a full-time stipendiary priest. She became more and more interested in worship and Anglicanism, and her life suddenly opened itself to the possibility of ordination. When the question was posed, she said Yes. Despite her fears that "a prophet is without honour in her home town," acceptance within her own community was phenomenal. Other local churches — United and Evangelical Lutheran Church in Canada — also called her to lead worship when they were without clergy. Michelle has taken numerous courses on subjects such as church history, tradition, liturgy, Bible study, pastoral care, ethics, and so on. She attended summer school at the College of Emmanuel and St. Chad in Saskatoon, and graduated from the four-year Education for Ministry (EFM) course. She currently leads worship twice a month in Manor and Cannington Manor churches, plus once a month in a nearby Lutheran church. She also works full time as a secretary. It is a very full schedule. Her secular job satisfies her monetary needs, and her work in the church satisfies a deeper spiritual requirement.

George Pell is an Anglican priest serving St. Peter's Ecumencial Church, an Anglican-Lutheran-United Shared Ministry in Slave Lake, Alberta, that celebrated its silver anniversary in 2001. He is married, with five grown children and stepchildren (but no grandchildren as yet). He has served in a variety of ministries both "inside" and "outside" the church: parish priest in the dioceses of Huron, Quebec, Calgary, and Athabasca; university-college chaplain in Quebec; YM–YWCA Child Services Director in Nova Scotia; and Community Services Director in Alberta. George has also served nine years as organist-musician-choir director in Anglican, Lutheran, and United churches, and began playing guitar when he led his first youth group. His ecumenical ventures began with involvement in diverse groups such as IVCF, Ontario English Catholic Teachers, Lay School of Theology, local study groups, Week of Prayer Events, and vacation church schools. His enthusiasm for music and sharing gifts has continued, and has brought him to his current ministry in Slave Lake.

Donald Phillips was born and raised in London, Ontario, where his family was one of the founding members of St. Michael and All

Angels parish. After marrying Nancy Rodgers, a fellow parishioner, and completing a Master of Science degree, he entered the Master of Divinity program at Huron College. Both he and Nancy were attracted to ministry in the North, where they spent seven years in the diocese of Athabasca. This "frontier" experience laid the foundation for his passion for educating and equipping all members of the church for ministry. After pastoring a new congregation in Fort McMurray, Alberta, he moved and became a parish incumbent, and then Diocesan Ministries Development Coordinator in the diocese of Qu'Appelle in southern Saskatchewan. In 2000, after eight years of diocesan ministry in Qu'Appelle (three of them as executive officer), he was elected as the twelfth bishop of Rupert's Land.

Dirk T. Rinehart-Pidcock grew up in a small eastern Oregon town, and has always had a deep affinity for small churches in rural landscapes. From l966–78 he served as a parish priest in three rural communities in the diocese of Eastern Oregon. The Total Ministry work of Bishop Wesley Frensdorff in the diocese of Nevada became an inspiration, having become rather disillusioned with conventional parish ministry. In 1978, he and his wife, Karen, and their three children moved to Sorrento Centre, where he served as director for six years, and focused on ministry development and the recovery of the ministry of the *laos*. Here their love affair with Canada matured. The next seven years found them at Christ Church Cathedral, Vancouver, where he learned much about working in partnership with gifted parish leaders. In l991, they moved to the Kokanee Region in the diocese of Kootenay, where he provided leadership for a Mutual Ministry initiative involving seven parishes. Six years later he was appointed Archdeacon of the Kootenays, with a mandate to assist parishes in the eastern portion of the diocese in ministry development initiatives. This past spring he ended his commitment as missioner for the Kokanee Region and continues a part-time ministry as archdeacon. Their home place, "Edensong," is in the lovely village of Kaslo, shared with a multitude of wild creatures, a friendly dog, cat, and a pair of bantam chickens.

Jack Risk has served as Program Coordinator for the diocese of Nova Scotia and PEI for five years. Previously, he facilitated a two-year ministry development project for a partnership of Anglican and non-Anglican parishes in South Burnaby, diocese of New Westminster. He was ordained in 1979, and served in rural and urban parishes in Saskatchewan for ten years. Jack's undergraduate work was in Art History. He received his MDiv from Trinity College, Toronto. Jack also holds an MA in Social Welfare Policy from McMaster University School of Social Work. His interests include zen, tai chi, gardening, and the critical theory of Jürgen Habermas. Jack is a parent of three, a step-parent of two, and a grandparent of one. He lives in Dartmouth, Nova Scotia, with his spouse, Christine.

Fletcher Stewart was born in England in the middle of World War II, and emigrated to Canada at age ten. He grew up in Scarborough, Ontario, where he came to Christ and was baptized in the Anglican Church. He attended Trinity College in Arts and Divinity during the 1960s, and met his wife, Pat, through the Student Christian Movement. He was ordained in 1968 in the diocese of Toronto, where he ministered in rural parishes for six years. Fletcher moved to Edmonton as an ecumenical university chaplain, where he lived for six years, and started work on his MTh at Newman College. (Thirteen years later, he finished his thesis, entitled *The Amelioration of Capitalism: The Corporate Responsibility Movement and the Transformation of Economic Life.*) In 1980, he moved to The Pas, Northern Manitoba, as rector of Christ Church, and in 1991, he moved down the road to the Henry Budd College for Ministry, where he is now coordinator. While in The Pas, he was a member of the Public Social Responsibility Unit, and the partners in Canadian Mission Unit, and was honoured to attend the Sacred Circle in Lethbridge in 1997.

Michael Thompson was recently appointed Principal Secretary to the Primate of the Anglican Church of Canada, following nine years as the incumbent of St. Cuthbert's Church, Toronto. He is a graduate of the University of Western Ontario (English Literature) and Trinity College, University of Toronto (MDiv and DMin). He is the co-author, with Paul MacLean, of *Seeking the Seeker*s (ABC Publishing, 2000), and contributes a regular column, "God Talk" to *PMC: The Practice of Ministry in Canada*. A co-founder of *Momentum*, the development program for newly ordained clergy in the diocese of Toronto, he has maintained an active interest in the characteristics of effective ordained ministry, and continues to serve as a facilitator in that program. He has coached kids' softball for the last eleven years, coming close to a championship only once.

Aileen Urquhart was born in Scotland, and grew up with a love of the land, the sea, and the hills. She spent time exploring the sacred places the stone circles and standing stones then formally studied biology, and followed a path of learning, teaching, and research in plant science. She worked in Wales, Ontario, then completed a PhD at Carleton University in Ottawa before she moved to Winnipeg.

An invitation to "try church" took her to Young United church, where community ministry was shared with All Saints Anglican church. It seemed to be a place "where the gospel was being lived." She began working in the inner city, and over the next ten years, encountered discrimination, prejudice, and a lack of opportunities for many disadvantaged groups, especially Indigenous people. She found support networks through ecumenical church and secular groups and, within herself, a commitment to social justice.

After further education in ministry, she was commissioned in 1994 as a diaconal minister in the United Church. Her first placement was in Fisher River, Manitoba, a small Indigenous reserve on the shores of Lake Winnipeg. At the Dr. Jessie Saulteaux Resource Centre, she participated in cross-cultural learning and student learning circles. In the fall of 1998, she accepted an interim position as co-director of the centre, while the Board searches for an Indigenous person to take on the role permanently.

FOR FURTHER READING

BAPTISM AND MINISTRY

Hill, John W.B. *Making Disciples: Serving Those Who Are Entering the Christian Life*. Toronto, Canada: Hoskin Group, 1991. 139 pages. A proposal for a restored catechumenate, built upon the vision of the *Book of Alternative Services*, calling us to reconsider the way we prepare people for baptism, and inviting us to begin from the baptismal rite itself.

Meyers, Ruth A., editor for the Standing Liturgical Commission. *Baptism and Ministry*. New York, NY: Church Hymnal Corporation, 1994. 102 pages. A collection of essays addressing the gradual shift in the church's understanding and practice of Christian initiation during the last century, and focusing on the growing awareness that the church's ministry belongs primarily to the baptized. The first in a series of *Liturgical Studies* issued under the direction of the Standing Liturgical Commission of the Episcopal Church of the USA.

World Council of Churches. *Baptism, Eucharist and Ministry*. Geneva: 1982. 33 pages. A formative study of the common understanding of baptism and ministry among member churches of the World Council of Churches.

A Theology of the Laity

Dozier, Verna J. II, editor. *The Calling of the Laity: Verna Dozier's Anthology.* Washington, DC: Alban Institute, 1988. vii, 149 pages. A collection of foundational and stirring essays by and about the laity and their sense of calling to ministry.

MacLean, Paul, and Michael Thompson. *Seeking the Seekers: Serving the Hidden Spiritual Quest.* Toronto, Canada: Anglican Book Centre, 1999. A study and guide about how to discover and respond to the spiritual needs of people both inside and outside the church.

Ordination and Orders

Countryman, L. William. *Living on the Border of the Holy: Renewing the Priesthood of All.* Harrisburg, Pennsylvania: Morehouse Publishing, 1999. xiii, 205 pages. Offers a way of understanding the priesthood of the whole people of God and the priesthood of the ordained by showing how both are rooted in the fundamental priestly nature of human life.

Plater, Ormonde. *Many Servants: An Introduction to Deacons.* Boston, Massachusetts: Cowley Publications, 1991. 213 pages. A lively and scholarly work on the role of the restored diaconate in the church today.

Local and Shared Ministry

Ellertson, Patricia. *Distinctive Thumbprints in Regional Ministry: Case Studies of Regional or Cluster Ministries.* Knoxville, Tennessee: Episcopal Appalachian Ministries, 1998. Additional copies of the booklet and study guide may be ordered from Episcopal Appalachian Ministries, Box 51931, Knoxville, Tennessee 37950-1931. Tel. 1-800-956-2776.

Greenwood, Robin. *The Ministry Team Handbook: Local Ministry as Partnership*. Great Britain: Society for Promoting Christian Knowledge, 2000. xxiii, 86 pages. Provides practical resources for groups of people who want to become a ministering community; to encourage a partnership between clergy and laity.

Zabriskie, Stewart C. *Total Ministry: Reclaiming the Ministry of All God's People*. Washington, DC: Alban Institute, 1995. 107 pages. A look at Total Ministry in the diocese of Nevada, providing theoretical, practical, testimonial, and biographical glimpses of a church where this model of ministry is thriving.

ABC Publishing
ANGLICAN BOOK CENTRE

SEEKING THE SEEKERS
Serving the Hidden Spiritual Quest
Paul MacLean and Michael Thompson
Using an approach that congregations can readily follow, the authors develop practical and effective strategies to reconnect with people's daily lives and inject new relevance into the church's mission.
1-55126-308-4 $16.95

ALIVE AGAIN
Recession and Recovery in our Churches
Reginald Stackhouse
In this fascinating study of "growth churches" across Canada, Stackhouse recounts real stories about real churches he has visited and considers the reasons for their exceptional growth.
1-55126-257-6 $16.95

ANGLICAN DIVERSITY
Challenges for the 21ˢᵗ Century
Patricia Bays takes a knowledgeable and sympathetic look at the Anglican Church today, and shows how diversity is its strength.
1-55126-327-0 $14.95

MOURNERS OR MIDWIVES
Choices for the 21st-Century Church
Lifetime Scholar Series, Course V
Herbert O'Driscoll
A richly illustrated look at human accomplishment—a scientific, artistic, social, and spiritual perspective—that encourages us to envision a realistic and vibrant future for Christianity and the church. Three-part video with study manual.
1-55126-231-2 $99.95

Available from your local bookstore or
Anglican Book Centre 1-800-268-1168
email: abc@national.anglican.ca Internet: www.abcpublishing.ca